THE GOSPEL ACCORDING TO LUKE

The Gospel According to

LUKE

With Notes
by Craig Munro

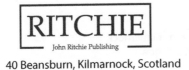

40 Beansburn, Kilmarnock, Scotland

ISBN-13: 978 1 912522 36 1

40 Beansburn, Kilmarnock, Scotland

www.ritchiechristianmedia.co.uk

Section headings taken from "What the Bible Teaches", John Heading.

Typeset by John Ritchie Ltd., Kilmarnock
Printed by Bell and Bain, Glasgow

Contents

Introduction 8
Chapter One 13
Chapter Two 19
Chapter Three 24
Chapter Four 28
Chapter Five 33
Chapter Sixb 37
Chapter Seven 42
Chapter Eight 47
Chapter Nine 53
Chapter Ten 59
Chapter Eleven 64
Chapter Twelve 69
Chapter Thirteen 75
Chapter Fourteen 79
Chapter Fifteen 83
Chapter Sixteen 87
Chapter Seventeen 91
Chapter Eighteen 95
Chapter Nineteen 99
Chapter Twenty 104
Chapter Twenty One 109
Chapter Twenty Two 113
Chapter Twenty Three 119
Chapter Twenty Four 124

The Gospel According to Luke

Dr Luke leaves us in no doubt why he wrote this Gospel: in the opening verses Luke states that he intends to set out an accurate and orderly record of the teaching, actions and life of the Lord Jesus Christ, the Son of God (Luke 1. 3). Luke wants the reader to have complete confidence in Christ. As a skilful historian he provides comprehensive evidence for the perfect humanity of Christ from His birth at Bethlehem to His death, resurrection and ascension in Jerusalem. He says to his friend Theophilus that he is writing this Gospel that he might *'know the certainty of those things, wherein thou hast been instructed'* (Luke 1. 4). This Gospel, therefore, is designed to introduce the reader to the greatest Man that has ever lived and to support believers in their relationship with Him as their Saviour.

The word 'Gospel' simply means good news and there are four gospel accounts of the life of Christ in the Bible – Matthew, Mark, Luke and John. The Bible itself is an amazing book. It is actually a library of sixty-six books written originally in three languages, on three continents and over a period of 1500 years, by kings, commoners, priests and prisoners. Amazingly, the message of each book is consistent with the whole. The Bible tells us of the greatness of God and His desire to bless mankind. We hope that after reading one of the books of the Bible you will want to read them all.

The four Gospels together provide a very full picture of the person and work of the Lord Jesus Christ. They are, however, not carbon copies of each other. Matthew, the converted tax collector, concentrates on proving to a Jewish audience that Christ was the Messiah, the Son of David, the true King. Mark sets out to prove that the Lord Jesus Christ was God's perfect Servant, emphasising the actions of Christ and the tireless energy that He exerted in His full and perfect service down here on earth. John, the fisherman, selects and describes for us a number of individuals who were initially unbelievers but who came to believe that Jesus was the Son of God and through believing in Him obtained eternal life.

Doctor Luke, on the other hand, stresses to a Gentile audience the perfect, holy, loving manhood of Christ. It is the Gospel of the common touch with many examples of the Lord Jesus in houses engaging people in eternal matters amidst the everyday events of family and social life. It is the Gospel where prayer, singing and worship are emphasised, in daily life, as well as temple service. The role of women in worship is particularly stressed in Luke's Gospel. It is also the Gospel where we find stories of personal salvation and the forgiveness of sins in almost every chapter. This Gospel also emphasises the importance of the Word of God for people of all nationalities. Luke writes his Gospel for the Gentile world. For example, he explains that Capernaum is a city of Galilee (Luke 4. 31). Luke interprets Jewish customs such as the Passover (Luke 22. 1) and substitutes Greek names for Hebrew names such as 'zealot' for 'Canaanite' (Luke 6. 15 c.f. Matthew 10. 4). Luke wanted his audience to fully understand the message about his Lord and Saviour, irrespective of their ethnicity, cultural background, or individual circumstances.

This Gospel of Luke is published with the prayer that you might receive Jesus Christ as your Lord and Saviour and receive forgiveness of sins. If you are already a Christian, this Gospel will also help you in your daily walk with God.

Marginal Notes

This Gospel is published with marginal notes for four reasons:

(1) This translation is the King James Version, first published in 1611. Some words need to be explained that are not in current use or that have changed their meaning.

(2) There are themes or thoughts that appear throughout the Gospel. Marginal comments allow the reader to trace some of these themes, and then re-examine the context and setting of each reference.

(3) Some biblical illustrations are not automatically understandable to a modern western mind and require explanation. Marginal comments of this nature are not frequent, as we believe Scripture should speak for itself.

(4) Luke has grouped his parables and miracles in a thematic order by the Holy Spirit to emphasise key points regarding the Lord's teaching and life. The theme in each chapter are in bold text at the start of each chapter in the notes. Some of these golden threads that connect the disparate acts, parables and teaching of Christ are outlined in the marginal notes.

Reflective Questions and Notes

A page with some reflective questions and a place to take notes is contained at the end of each chapter. These pages are designed to provoke thought and to encourage the reader to pause, take notes and reflect in their personal daily readings, to facilitate discussion in small group Bible studies, and for use in personal evangelism. Some texts are highlighted by red text as a suggested possible verse or verses for memorisation.

The Sower of the Seed

A sower went out to sow his seed: and as he sowed, some fell by the way side; and it was trodden down, and the fowls of the air devoured it. And some fell upon a rock; and as soon as it was sprung up, it withered away, because it lacked moisture. And some fell among thorns; and the thorns sprang up with it, and choked it. And other fell on good ground, and sprang up, and bare fruit an hundredfold. And when he had said these things, he cried, He that hath ears to hear, let him hear. And his disciples asked him, saying, What might this parable be? And he said, Unto you it is given to know the mysteries of the kingdom of God: but to others in parables; that seeing they might not see, and hearing they might not understand Now the parable is this: ***The seed is the word of God.*** *Those by the way side are they that hear; then cometh the devil, and taketh away the word out of their hearts,* ***lest they should believe and be saved.*** *They on the rock are they, which, when they hear, receive the word with joy; and these have no root, which for a while believe, and in time of temptation fall away. And that which fell among thorns are they, which, when they have heard, go forth, and are choked with cares and riches and pleasures of this life, and bring no fruit to perfection. But that on the good ground are they, which in an honest and good heart, having heard the word, keep it, and bring forth fruit with patience (Luke 8. 5-15).*

The Seed is the Word of God – the miracle of eternal life

The Lord Jesus was not giving a biology lesson about seed in the parable of the Sower but He was teaching a spiritual lesson. He transferred the idea of sowing seed in soil to sowing the seed of His own word – the Word of God. The biological life contained within seed allowing plants to germinate, grow, flower and bloom, is compared with people accepting the living Word of God, developing, growing and bringing some beauty to God in a sinful world. We have in our hands the very Word of God. But to have this life-giving effect upon us, the Word of God must be received into our hearts just as the soil must receive the seed.

The four different soil types illustrate the four attitudes and mindsets of the hearers to the Word of God. All readers must decide which category of hearer they fit into.

1. The wayside – The uncaring or unconcerned hearer of the gospel (v12)

The seed at the wayside is "trodden down" because it lies at the sides of the field. This is a picture of people who have little care for their soul's salvation and they oppose the message of Christ and deliberately or unwittingly tread down the Word of God in their hearts. They are unaware that the Devil delights in their attitude and the illustration of the birds picking up the seed is a picture of the power of Satan using their attitude to stop them giving the matter of their soul's salvation second thoughts *'lest they should believe and be saved'*.

2. The stony ground – the unthinking hearer of the gospel (v13)

When the seed lands in the stony soil it flourishes initially but soon dies as it has no root. The soil is too thinly spread in the stony ground and the root cannot source any moisture. It is a picture of someone who hears the message of the gospel and seems to be attracted to it and without counting the cost or repenting of sins professes to be saved. However, they do not have the root of the matter, they have never really repented of their sin, and were never prepared to take Christ as Lord of their life. They still loved their old way of life too much. Whenever the demands of the discipleship of Christ are made upon them they are shown to be what they are – dead to God.

3. The thorny ground – the unaffected hearer of the gospel (v14)

In this soil, the seed hardly touches the ground before the thorns surround it and block the light source and suck up the moisture and generally give the little seed no chance to germinate and grow. The thorns, the Saviour said, were the *'cares, riches and pleasures of this life'*. This is the hearer of the gospel who is not rude or opposed to the message. They will listen, but they believe there are more important things to be worried about such as health, family, or pleasures. Life to them does not have to be quite so serious. They like pursuing their pleasures and sins. The truth of the matter is that these things occupy the listener's mind and block out the life source -Christ. They are walking down the broad road of life with all the cares of this life on their shoulders; these listeners are discontented, chasing sinful pleasure and tragically unaware that it leads to destruction.

4. The good ground – the fruitful hearer of the gospel (v15)

The seed of the Word of God now lands on good soil, germinates, grows, and brings forth fruit. These are the people who having heard the Word of God, obey it and bring pleasure in their life to God. They listen to what God is saying to them. They allow the impact of God's Word to enter their heart. They repent of their sin and open their lives to Christ as Saviour and Lord understanding that He has died for them on the cross. They enter into a living fruitful relationship with Him knowing that He is alive having been raised again from the dead. Just as the seed in good soil shows it has life so they show that they have eternal life. They can now bring God some pleasure in their life here and now, and in a day to come will be in heaven with their Saviour.

As we read the words of Christ in Luke's Gospel, we need to ask ourselves the question - which type of soil represents my position? Everyone's heart can be good ground. The Lord Jesus said, *'Repent , and believe the gospel'* (Mark 1. 15) and again *'except ye repent, ye shall all likewise perish'* (Luke 13. 3).

Luke 1

Preface and the Purpose of the Book

1 Forasmuch as many have taken in hand to set forth in order a declaration of those things which are most surely believed among us,
2 Even as they delivered them unto us, which from the beginning were eyewitnesses, and ministers of the word;
3 It seemed good to me also, having had perfect understanding of all things from the very first, to write unto thee in order, most excellent Theophilus,
4 That thou mightest know the certainty of those things, wherein thou hast been instructed.

The Birth of John the Baptist Foretold

5 There was in the days of Herod, the king of Judaea, a certain priest named Zacharias, of the course of Abia: and his wife was of the daughters of Aaron, and her name was Elisabeth.
6 And they were both righteous before God, walking in all the commandments and ordinances of the Lord blameless.
7 And they had no child, because that Elisabeth was barren, and they both were now well stricken in years.
8 And it came to pass, that while he executed the priest's office before God in the order of his course,
9 According to the custom of the priest's office, his lot was to burn incense when he went into the temple of the Lord.
10 And the whole multitude of the people were praying without at the time of incense.
11 And there appeared unto him an angel of the Lord standing on the right side of the altar of incense.
12 And when Zacharias saw him, he was troubled, and fear fell upon him.
13 But the angel said unto him, Fear not, Zacharias: for thy prayer is heard; and thy wife Elisabeth shall bear thee a son, and thou shalt call his name John.
14 And thou shalt have joy and gladness; and many shall rejoice at his birth.

Chapter 1 The Birth of John the Baptist and the announcing of the Christ.

1.1 Many people had recorded the sayings and works of the Christ of God which could be substantiated by living witnesses and sincerely believed amongst all followers of Christ.
1.2 Those who recorded them were eye witnesses and had first hand experience of what they wrote down.
1.3 Luke is stating that he too has a full understanding of all these things and he wants to set out in a permanent and orderly form so that the man he was writing to, Theophilus, and all others after him would have an accurate record of the teaching and actions of Christ.
1.4 We do not know who Theophilus was, clearly a prominent Christian, but Luke, a medical doctor (Col. 4.14), wanted to assure him of the evidence and certainty of those things which he had believed.
1.5 Luke's time notes are very important. He is an accurate historian. His details could be checked up.
1.7 'well stricken in years' – means they were old.
1.8 'in the order' – that is the order or 'course' referred to in 1.5. The priest took in turns (orders) to serve in the temple (see 1 Chronicles 25).
1.9-10. Prayer is always associated with the incense offered up on the Golden altar (Rev. 5. 8, 8. 3). The prayers of God's people are regarded as incense in heaven.
1.11 In the temple the altar of incense was directly in front of the veil into the Holiest of All.
1.12 'Troubled' means 'anxious'.
1.13 'Thy prayer is heard' – see Acts 10.31. God hears the prayers of those that fear Him.

1.15 This absence of alcohol is a reference to the special vow in the law of the Nazarite in Numbers 6. 3.

1.16 A prophecy regarding the success of the child's future call as a preacher; the child would become known as John the Baptist.

1.17 'Elias' means Elijah (1 Kings 17. 1). 'Hearts of the fathers to the children' – means that the older men who had perhaps lost hope now have a child-like faith and joy.

1.18 Zacharias the Priest doubts that it is physically possible given his age and the age of his wife to have a child. 'Well stricken' literally means 'getting on' translated 'great age' in 2.36.

1.20 This lack of faith to believe God's Word brought about a judgment of dumbness.

1.21 'marvelled' means 'surprised'; 'tarried' means 'waited'.

1.23 'days of his ministration' – the short period of time each year allotted to him as Priest to function in the temple.

1.25 Elizabeth regards her pregnancy to be from God and removed the cruel reproach she felt from others for having no children.

1.26 Nazareth is a small town in northern Israel about 65 miles north of Jerusalem.

1.27 'espoused' – this means that Mary was 'betrothed' to Joseph, an ancient Jewish system of promising to marry someone which was legally binding but where the couple were not

15 For he shall be great in the sight of the Lord, and
shall drink neither wine nor strong drink; and he
shall be filled with the Holy Ghost, even from his
mother's womb.
16 And many of the children of Israel shall he turn
to the Lord their God.
17 And he shall go before him in the spirit and power
of Elias, to turn the hearts of the fathers to the
children, and the disobedient to the wisdom of the
just; to make ready a people prepared for the Lord.
18 And Zacharias said unto the angel, Whereby shall
I know this? for I am an old man, and my wife well
stricken in years.
19 And the angel answering said unto him, I am
Gabriel, that stand in the presence of God; and am
sent to speak unto thee, and to shew thee these
glad tidings.
20 And, behold, thou shalt be dumb, and not able
to speak, until the day that these things shall be
performed, because thou believest not my words,
which shall be fulfilled in their season.
21 And the people waited for Zacharias, and
marvelled that he tarried so long in the temple.
22 And when he came out, he could not speak unto
them: and they perceived that he had seen a vision
in the temple: for he beckoned unto them, and
remained speechless.
23 And it came to pass, that, as soon as the days of
his ministration were accomplished, he departed
to his own house.
24 And after those days his wife Elisabeth conceived,
and hid herself five months, saying,
25 Thus hath the Lord dealt with me in the days
wherein he looked on me, to take away my reproach
among men.

The Promise of the Birth of the Lord Jesus

26 And in the sixth month the angel Gabriel was sent
from God unto a city of Galilee, named Nazareth,
27 To a virgin espoused to a man whose name was
Joseph, of the house of David; and the virgin's name
was Mary.
28 And the angel came in unto her, and said, Hail,

thou that art highly favoured, the Lord is with thee: blessed art thou among women.
29 And when she saw him, she was troubled at his saying, and cast in her mind what manner of salutation this should be.
30 And the angel said unto her, Fear not, Mary: for thou hast found favour with God.
31 And, behold, thou shalt conceive in thy womb, and bring forth a son, and shalt call his name Jesus.
32 He shall be great, and shall be called the Son of the Highest: and the Lord God shall give unto him the throne of his father David:
33 And he shall reign over the house of Jacob for ever; and of his kingdom there shall be no end.
34 Then said Mary unto the angel, How shall this be, seeing I know not a man?
35 And the angel answered and said unto her, The Holy Ghost shall come upon thee, and the power of the Highest shall overshadow thee: therefore also that holy thing which shall be born of thee shall be called the Son of God.
36 And, behold, thy cousin Elisabeth, she hath also conceived a son in her old age: and this is the sixth month with her, who was called barren.
37 For with God nothing shall be impossible.
38 And Mary said, Behold the handmaid of the Lord; be it unto me according to thy word. And the angel departed from her.

The Visit of Mary to Elizabeth and Mary's Praise

39 And Mary arose in those days, and went into the hill country with haste, into a city of Juda;
40 And entered into the house of Zacharias, and saluted Elisabeth.
41 And it came to pass, that, when Elisabeth heard the salutation of Mary, the babe leaped in her womb; and Elisabeth was filled with the Holy Ghost:
42 And she spake out with a loud voice, and said, Blessed art thou among women, and blessed is the fruit of thy womb.
43 And whence is this to me, that the mother of my Lord should come to me?
44 For, lo, as soon as the voice of thy salutation

actually married yet. Sexual relations had not taken place. They were virgins.

1.28 'Hail' means 'Rejoice'.

1.29 'manner of salutation' means 'type of greeting'.

1.31 'Jesus' means 'Saviour' (Matt. 1.21)

1.32 'Son' is not a child in Hebrew thought. It speaks of character and dignity and not so much of birth or lineage. 'The Highest' – a title for the greatness of God. 'David' – Israel's greatest king. The child was divine and was the Messiah – the anointed King.

1.33 'no end' – an eternal kingdom

1.34 'know not a man' – a euphemism for 'I have never had sexual relations and do not intend to until I am married'.

1.35 Mary's baby is to be divinely conceived with no human involvement as the prophet Isaiah had foretold the Messiah would be (Isa. 7.14). God would become a child.

1.36 The angel informs Mary about her cousin Elizabeth back in Jerusalem who has conceived naturally, but is actually very old.

1.37 an incredible statement about God's omnipotence!

1.38 Mary believes and accepts and takes the place of being a servant (handmaid) to Jehovah God, ready to do His will.

1.41-42 These two women unite in joy knowing that God is working in their lives in a miraculous way. John the Baptist will be born first to herald in the Christ of God.

1.43 'whence is this to me' means 'why is this granted to me?'

1.44 'salutation' means greeting.

sounded in mine ears, the babe leaped in my womb for joy.

45 And blessed is she that believed: for there shall be a performance of those things which were told her from the Lord.

1.45 'Blessed is she that believed' – this is a rule of life for the believer.

46 And Mary said, My soul doth magnify the Lord,

1.46 This song is often called the Magnificat. Mary magnifies the Lord.

47 And my spirit hath rejoiced in God my Saviour.

1.47 Mary rejoices in God as Saviour.

48 For he hath regarded the low estate of his handmaiden: for, behold, from henceforth all generations shall call me blessed.

1.48 Mary rejoices in the God of Grace stooping down to the 'low estate of his handmaiden' i.e. the low social state of her as a maidservant.

49 For he that is mighty hath done to me great things; and holy is his name.

1.49 Mary rejoices in the greatness and goodness of God.

50 And his mercy is on them that fear him from generation to generation.

1.50 Mary rejoices in the mercy of God.

51 He hath shewed strength with his arm; he hath scattered the proud in the imagination of their hearts.

1.51 Mary rejoices in the righteous judgment and actions of God.

52 He hath put down the mighty from their seats, and exalted them of low degree.

1.52 'exalted' literally means 'lifted up' in contrast to those He 'put down'. The words 'low degree' just means 'lowly'.

53 He hath filled the hungry with good things; and the rich he hath sent empty away.

1.53 Mary rejoices in the compassion of God.

54 He hath holpen his servant Israel, in remembrance of his mercy;

55 As he spake to our fathers, to Abraham, and to his seed for ever.

1.55 'spake' means 'spoke'.

56 And Mary abode with her about three months, and returned to her own house.

1.56 – see verse 36. Mary returns in the ninth month of Elisabeth's pregnancy.

The Birth of John

57 Now Elisabeth's full time came that she should be delivered; and she brought forth a son.

1.57 The baby is called John the Baptist who was born 6 months before the Christ (v36, v56).

58 And her neighbours and her cousins heard how the Lord had shewed great mercy upon her; and they rejoiced with her.

1.58 'shewed' means 'showed'.

59 And it came to pass, that on the eighth day they came to circumcise the child; and they called him Zacharias, after the name of his father.

1.59 Jewish tradition on the eighth day is to cut away the foreskin of the male child (Gen 17. 10-13).

60 And his mother answered and said, Not so; but he shall be called John.

61 And they said unto her, There is none of thy kindred that is called by this name.

1.61 'kindred' means 'family'.

62 And they made signs to his father, how he would have him called.

1.62 Non-verbal communication continues – see v22.

63 And he asked for a writing table, and wrote, saying, His name is John. And they marvelled all.
64 And his mouth was opened immediately, and his tongue loosed, and he spake, and praised God.
65 And fear came on all that dwelt round about them: and all these sayings were noised abroad throughout all the hill country of Judaea.
66 And all they that heard them laid them up in their hearts, saying, What manner of child shall this be! And the hand of the Lord was with him.

The Song of Zacharias

67 And his father Zacharias was filled with the Holy Ghost, and prophesied, saying,
68 Blessed be the Lord God of Israel; for he hath visited and redeemed his people,
69 And hath raised up an horn of salvation for us in the house of his servant David;
70 As he spake by the mouth of his holy prophets, which have been since the world began:
71 That we should be saved from our enemies, and from the hand of all that hate us;
72 To perform the mercy promised to our fathers, and to remember his holy covenant;
73 The oath which he sware to our father Abraham,
74 That he would grant unto us, that we being delivered out of the hand of our enemies might serve him without fear,
75 In holiness and righteousness before him, all the days of our life.
76 And thou, child, shalt be called the prophet of the Highest: for thou shalt go before the face of the Lord to prepare his ways;
77 To give knowledge of salvation unto his people by the remission of their sins,
78 Through the tender mercy of our God; whereby the dayspring from on high hath visited us,
79 To give light to them that sit in darkness and in the shadow of death, to guide our feet into the way of peace.
80 And the child grew, and waxed strong in spirit, and was in the deserts till the day of his shewing unto Israel.

1.63 His Name 'is' John and not 'should be called' John. Zacharias had got the name from the angel (v13) and nothing would alter his view – not even family tradition (v61).

1.64 'tongue loosed' – spoke freely.

1.65 'noised abroad' – discussed openly.

1.66 'what manner' means 'what sort' of child is this that has been born?

1.67 'Holy Ghost' means 'Holy Spirit' – a divine Person in the Triune God. God the Father, God the Son and God the Holy Spirit (Matthew 28.19).

1.68 'redeemed' means to purchase with a view to deliver from slavery (v74).

1.69 'horn of salvation' is a figure of speech that speaks of the power of God's salvation.

1.70 'holy prophets' – people like Moses, Isaiah, Jeremiah etc.

1.72 'holy covenant' is a reminder of a solemn promise to Abraham by God about the land of Israel (Genesis 15).

1.76 'prophet of the Highest' – the Highest is a Name for the Christ of God. John would be the forerunner ('shall go before the face of the Lord') for the Christ.

1.77 Salvation is the remission (literally the 'letting go'), the release or forgiveness from our sins.

1.78 Salvation is love. The 'day spring from on high' – the rising sun, the morning light. A figure of the warmth of God's kindness in Christ in coming down to us here on earth.

1.79 Salvation is light and liberty: peace with God.

1.80 'waxed strong' – means 'became strong'.
'deserts' - John had a rural upbringing.

Reflective Questions and Notes

A. Why is Luke writing this Gospel? (see v1-4)

B. Why did Zacharias doubt God's ability to give his wife a child? (v18)

C. How was Mary informed that she would have a child although still a virgin? (v31-37)

D. What was prophesied to be the role and purpose in life for the child that would become known as John the Baptist? (v76-80)

Luke 2

The Birth of the Lord Jesus

1 And it came to pass in those days, that there went
out a decree from Caesar Augustus that all the world
should be taxed.
2 (And this taxing was first made when Cyrenius was
governor of Syria.)
3 And all went to be taxed, every one into his own
city.
4 And Joseph also went up from Galilee, out of the
city of Nazareth, into Judaea, unto the city of David,
which is called Bethlehem; (because he was of the
house and lineage of David:)
5 To be taxed with Mary his espoused wife, being
great with child.
6 And so it was, that, while they were there, the days
were accomplished that she should be delivered.
7 And she brought forth her firstborn son, and
wrapped him in swaddling clothes, and laid him
in a manger; because there was no room for them
in the inn.

The Message of the Angels to the Shepherds

8 And there were in the same country shepherds
abiding in the field, keeping watch over their flock
by night.
9 And, lo, the angel of the Lord came upon them,
and the glory of the Lord shone round about them:
and they were sore afraid.
10 And the angel said unto them, Fear not: for,
behold, I bring you good tidings of great joy, which
shall be to all people.
11 For unto you is born this day in the city of David
a Saviour, which is Christ the Lord.
12 And this shall be a sign unto you; Ye shall find
the babe wrapped in swaddling clothes, lying in a
manger.
13 And suddenly there was with the angel a
multitude of the heavenly host praising God, and
saying,
14 Glory to God in the highest, and on earth peace,
good will toward men.

Chapter 2 The birth of Christ

2.1 Caesar was the ruler of the Roman Empire. At that time Israel was ruled by Rome. Caesar wanted to know how many people there were in each part of his kingdom, with a view to increasing taxation and contol over the people.

2.2 Taxation was relatively common in the Roman era. This is a historical comment from Luke telling us when this particular tax took place.

2.3 This taxing or enrolment demanded people to go to the place of their birth which must have resulted in mass movement across the empire.

2.4 The result of this big decision in Rome was that Joseph had to go to Bethlehem.

2.5 Joseph had to take Mary as he is now 'espoused' that is 'betrothed' to Mary, which is not marriage, but it was legally binding unlike 'engagement' today. Mary, for example, is referred to as Joseph's wife even although they are not living together and are still virgins.

2.6 Therefore the Christ was born in Bethlehem, just as the prophet hundreds of years before had foretold (Micah 5. 2). Caesar's tax plan, without knowing it, was part of God's greater plan.

2.7 The first clothes for the Saviour were strips of cloth. The first bed was an animal's eating trough. What humility! What grace! The inn keeper had no room for the Saviour. It is the same today.

2.9 'Lo' means 'behold, see'. 'Sore afraid' means 'filled with fear'.

2.10 Shepherds are the first to hear the wonderful news that God has come into the world as a baby. He has come for all people.

2.11 'A Saviour' – just what we all need. One that can save us from our sins, an empty life and

from God's judgment. 'Christ' is a Greek word meaning 'anointed', the Hebrew equivalent word is 'Messiah'. 'Lord' – all must obey Him.
2.13 What must it have been to hear the choirs of angels praise God? The song of creation would have been special but the song of the incarnation (God becoming a man) must have been incredible.
2.14 They sang of glory to God first and the outcome of this is peace to the human race.
2.16 How fitting that the shepherds were the first to see the Christ in such humble circumstances. Here was One who would be the 'good Shepherd that would give His life for the sheep' (John 10.11).
2.17 They could not stop telling others about Him. This is what happens when people come to see Christ for Who He really is.
2.18 Others became curious and some became believers in the Lord Jesus by the testimony of the shepherds alone.
2.19 Mary had a private and personal faith in Christ which was deep. She enjoyed meditating upon Him. Christians still do.
2.20 Believing in the Lord Jesus always results in worship: 'glorifying and praising God'.
2.21 For explanation of circumcision see 1.5 9.
Jesus means 'Saviour' (Matthew 1.21)
2.22 This would be on the fortieth day after the birth (Leviticus 12. 1-4).
What a statement: 'presenting Him - 'the Lord' (2. 11) - to the Lord'. The Bible teaches that there is one God but He is manifested in three persons – God the Father, God the Son and God the Holy Spirit (Matthew 28. 19).
2.24 Leviticus 12 teaches us that it was only the poor that brought birds for sacrifice. The Lord Jesus was born into a poor home.

15 And it came to pass, as the angels were gone
away from them into heaven, the shepherds said
one to another, Let us now go even unto Bethlehem,
and see this thing which is come to pass, which the
Lord hath made known unto us.
16 And they came with haste, and found Mary, and
Joseph, and the babe lying in a manger.
17 And when they had seen it, they made known
abroad the saying which was told them concerning
this child.
18 And all they that heard it wondered at those
things which were told them by the shepherds.
19 But Mary kept all these things, and pondered
them in her heart.
20 And the shepherds returned, glorifying and
praising God for all the things that they had heard
and seen, as it was told unto them.

The Circumcision and Naming of the Lord

21 And when eight days were accomplished for the
circumcising of the child, his name was called Jesus,
which was so named of the angel before he was
conceived in the womb.
22 And when the days of her purification according
to the law of Moses were accomplished, they
brought him to Jerusalem, to present him to the
Lord;
23 (As it is written in the law of the Lord, Every
male that openeth the womb shall be called holy
to the Lord;)
24 And to offer a sacrifice according to that which
is said in the law of the Lord, A pair of turtledoves,
or two young pigeons.

The Godly Simeon and His Prophesy

25 And, behold, there was a man in Jerusalem,
whose name was Simeon; and the same man was
just and devout, waiting for the consolation of Israel:
and the Holy Ghost was upon him.
26 And it was revealed unto him by the Holy Ghost,
that he should not see death, before he had seen
the Lord's Christ.
27 And he came by the Spirit into the temple: and

when the parents brought in the child Jesus, to do
for him after the custom of the law,
28 Then took he him up in his arms, and blessed
God, and said,
29 Lord, now lettest thou thy servant depart in
peace, according to thy word:
30 For mine eyes have seen thy salvation,
31 Which thou hast prepared before the face of all
people;
32 A light to lighten the Gentiles, and the glory of
thy people Israel.
33 And Joseph and his mother marvelled at those
things which were spoken of him.
34 And Simeon blessed them, and said unto Mary
his mother, Behold, this child is set for the fall and
rising again of many in Israel; and for a sign which
shall be spoken against;
35 (Yea, a sword shall pierce through thy own soul
also,) that the thoughts of many hearts may be
revealed.

Anna, "She Spake of Him"

36 And there was one Anna, a prophetess, the
daughter of Phanuel, of the tribe of Aser: she was
of a great age, and had lived with an husband seven
years from her virginity;
37 And she was a widow of about fourscore and
four years, which departed not from the temple, but
served God with fastings and prayers night and day.
38 And she coming in that instant gave thanks
likewise unto the Lord, and spake of him to all them
that looked for redemption in Jerusalem.

The Silent Years at Nazareth

39 And when they had performed all things
according to the law of the Lord, they returned into
Galilee, to their own city Nazareth.
40 And the child grew, and waxed strong in spirit,
filled with wisdom: and the grace of God was upon
him.

The Boy of Twelve in the Temple

41 Now his parents went to Jerusalem every year at
the feast of the passover.

2.25 'consolation of Israel' – a Hebrew expression having its roots in comfort and solace but referring to the salvation that will come to Israel with the coming Messiah.

2.26 Simeon was fully expecting to see the Christ before he died as revealed to him by the Holy Spirit.

2.28 Simeon held the Christ of God in His arms.

2.29 'Lord, now lettest' means 'Lord, now You are letting'. Simeon knew he now would die as he had seen the face of the Christ of God.

2.31 God's salvation is for all people – no exceptions.

2.32 God's salvation is for Jewish people and non-Jewish people (Gentiles).

2.33 – See verse 19. Mary and Joseph are increasing in wonder at what they are learning about the child.

2.34 Simeon begins to prophesy that the Christ will be spoken against by those who do not believe. 'Rising again of many' – to those who believe, Christ will bless with salvation and inspire, others who reject Him will 'fall' in judgment.

2.35 Simeon warns that Mary will witness the rejection of Christ bringing sorrow to her soul. The 'piercing' is the first suggestion of His crucifixion.

2.36 'Aser' is 'Asher' (Gen. 49.20) one of Jacob's sons. Anna is an old widow, her husband died seven years after the wedding and she did not remarry.

2.37 'Fourscore and four years' means 84 years. A woman of prayer.

2.38 'coming in that instant' – she arrived as Simeon is holding the Christ. 'Redemption' – this is a legal word that speaks of a ransom price paid and deliverance from bondage. Anna is claiming that the child is the Redeemer.

2.39 Nazareth – is about 65 miles north in Galilee (see 2.4).

2.40 At every stage of His

development He brought pleasure to God.

2.41 The Passover feast was always on the 14 day of the first month of the year around our March/April. It celebrated Israel's deliverance from Egypt.

2.43 'fulfilled the days' – they would stay for a week as the feast of Unleavened Bread ran on immediately after the Passover for seven days (Lev. 23.5-6).

2.44 Mary and Joseph assumed he was with the extended family on the journey home but the Lord Jesus was still in Jerusalem. Is it possible that we can journey through life assuming He is with us?

2.46 'Three days' – one day journey away, another journey back and on the third day they found Him in the temple sitting amongst the 'doctors' of the law, the acknowledged experts in the Scriptures.

2.47 Everyone was astonished at His superior knowledge of Scripture even as a boy of twelve.

2.49 'Wist ye not' – means 'Did you not understand?'.

'My Father's business' – speaking of the eternal relationship between the Father and the Son of God.

2.51 Wonder of wonders. God became a man, and then became subject to His earthly parents keeping commandment number 5: 'honour thy father and thy mother'. Brought up in a lowly town in northern Israel. What grace!

2.52 At every stage of life He brought glory to God.

42 And when he was twelve years old, they went up to Jerusalem after the custom of the feast.

43 And when they had fulfilled the days, as they returned, the child Jesus tarried behind in Jerusalem; and Joseph and his mother knew not of it.

44 But they, supposing him to have been in the company, went a day's journey; and they sought him among their kinsfolk and acquaintance.

45 And when they found him not, they turned back again to Jerusalem, seeking him.

46 And it came to pass, that after three days they found him in the temple, sitting in the midst of the doctors, both hearing them, and asking them questions.

47 And all that heard him were astonished at his understanding and answers.

48 And when they saw him, they were amazed: and his mother said unto him, Son, why hast thou thus dealt with us? behold, thy father and I have sought thee sorrowing.

49 And he said unto them, How is it that ye sought me? wist ye not that I must be about my Father's business?

50 And they understood not the saying which he spake unto them.

51 And he went down with them, and came to Nazareth, and was subject unto them: but his mother kept all these sayings in her heart.

52 And Jesus increased in wisdom and stature, and in favour with God and man.

Reflective Questions and Notes

A. What brought Mary and Joseph to Bethlehem? (v1-4) Why is this fascinating? (v6 margin)

B. What is the effect of the birth of Christ on angels and people? (v13, 20)

C. What had been revealed to Simeon? (v26)

D. What are the first recorded words of Christ in Luke's gospel at the age of twelve? (v49)

____

____

____

____

____

Chapter 3 The baptism of Christ

3.1 Luke gives us incredible historical detail of the political leaders at this time and great accuracy in the titles that they were given. Judea is south Israel; Galilee is north Israel; Ituraea – north of Galilee, part of present day Syria; Abilene is part of modern day Lebanon. The fifteenth year of Tiberius Caesar is reckoned to be AD29 as Tiberius reigned from AD 14 to AD 37. This gives us a very accurate date for the start of John the Baptist's ministry.

3.3 John had a very simple message – repentance. That is completely forsake your sins and turn to God if you wish to be forgiven. This was expressed in baptism.

3.4-6 Esaias is a transliteration of 'Isaiah' the prophet. This quotation is taken from Isaiah 40.3-4 some 700 years before John was born. John was to be the forerunner to the Christ preparing the way for Christ. ('the salvation of God').

3.7 John did not pander to his audience! He was bold and called them out for their sins and warned of coming judgment.

3.8 John wanted to see reality! He was particularly against people assuming that their birth or ethnicity (in this case their link to Abraham) somehow gave them favour with God.

3.9 The Gospel is like an axe to a tree, bringing down all pride. A true relationship with God is brought out by repentance for our sins and faith in Christ alone.

3.11 The Gospel not only forgives sins but changes our behaviour – giving freely of our possessions to others in need.

Luke 3

The Ministry of John the Baptist

1 Now in the fifteenth year of the reign of Tiberius Caesar, Pontius Pilate being governor of Judaea, and Herod being tetrarch of Galilee, and his brother Philip tetrarch of Ituraea and of the region of Trachonitis, and Lysanias the tetrarch of Abilene,
2 Annas and Caiaphas being the high priests, the word of God came unto John the son of Zacharias in the wilderness.
3 And he came into all the country about Jordan, preaching the baptism of repentance for the remission of sins;
4 As it is written in the book of the words of Esaias the prophet, saying, The voice of one crying in the wilderness, Prepare ye the way of the Lord, make his paths straight.
5 Every valley shall be filled, and every mountain and hill shall be brought low; and the crooked shall be made straight, and the rough ways shall be made smooth;
6 And all flesh shall see the salvation of God.
7 Then said he to the multitude that came forth to be baptized of him, O generation of vipers, who hath warned you to flee from the wrath to come?
8 Bring forth therefore fruits worthy of repentance, and begin not to say within yourselves, We have Abraham to our father: for I say unto you, That God is able of these stones to raise up children unto Abraham.
9 And now also the axe is laid unto the root of the trees: every tree therefore which bringeth not forth good fruit is hewn down, and cast into the fire.
10 And the people asked him, saying, What shall we do then?
11 He answereth and saith unto them, He that hath two coats, let him impart to him that hath none; and he that hath meat, let him do likewise.
12 Then came also publicans to be baptized, and said unto him, Master, what shall we do?
13 And he said unto them, Exact no more than that which is appointed you.

14 And the soldiers likewise demanded of him, saying, And what shall we do? And he said unto them, Do violence to no man, neither accuse any falsely; and be content with your wages.
15 And as the people were in expectation, and all men mused in their hearts of John, whether he were the Christ, or not;
16 John answered, saying unto them all, I indeed baptize you with water; but one mightier than I cometh, the latchet of whose shoes I am not worthy to unloose: he shall baptize you with the Holy Ghost and with fire:
17 Whose fan is in his hand, and he will throughly purge his floor, and will gather the wheat into his garner; but the chaff he will burn with fire unquenchable.
18 And many other things in his exhortation preached he unto the people.
19 But Herod the tetrarch, being reproved by him for Herodias his brother Philip's wife, and for all the evils which Herod had done,
20 Added yet this above all, that he shut up John in prison.

The Baptism of the Lord Jesus

21 Now when all the people were baptized, it came to pass, that Jesus also being baptized, and praying, the heaven was opened,
22 And the Holy Ghost descended in a bodily shape like a dove upon him, and a voice came from heaven, which said, Thou art my beloved Son; in thee I am well pleased.

The Genealogy of the Lord Jesus

23 And Jesus himself began to be about thirty years of age, being (as was supposed) the son of Joseph, which was the son of Heli,
24 Which was the son of Matthat, which was the son of Levi, which was the son of Melchi, which was the son of Janna, which was the son of Joseph,
25 Which was the son of Mattathias, which was the son of Amos, which was the son of Naum, which was the son of Esli, which was the son of Nagge,
26 Which was the son of Maath, which was the son

3.12 'publicans' – means tax collectors.

3.13 The gospel demanded that the tax collectors were honest.

3.14 The Gospel demanded that the soldiers were not abusive and violent, but upright and contented.

3.15 The people expected the coming Messiah from the Old Testament Scriptures and wondered ('mused') if John was that person.

3.16 John assures that he is not the Christ. Indeed he was not worthy of being a servant to Christ, for example, even taking the sandals off his feet.

3.17 John informs us that the Christ is a Saviour and can baptise with the Holy Spirit and produce a divine work in all who believe. He also will be one day a judge who will judge the unbeliever with fire. 'chaff' - stubble left over after harvest.

3.19 Herod– a ruler of Galilee (3.1) a quarter (meaning of the word 'tetrarch') of the whole area now known as Israel, Lebanon, Syria.

3.19-20 Herod took the wife of his brother Philip which is shocking even by today's standards. John rebuked him for his sin and as a result was imprisoned.

3.21 The baptism of the Lord Jesus was different to all other baptisms. All others involved them confessing sin, but He confessed righteousness (Matthew 3. 14-15). It was uniquely at the baptism of Christ that God spoke directly from heaven and the Holy Spirit was seen to descend as a dove.

3.23 For thirty years He had lived a quiet, holy life in Galilee. Now He would preach to the world.

3.24-38. This genealogy should

be read along with Matthew 1. Matthew's genealogy goes back via David to Abraham. It seeks to prove Christ's right to the throne and the land. Matthew proves the Lord Jesus was no actual son of Joseph (not of the cursed line of Jeconiah) but was the actual son of Mary, but still had the legal right to the throne through Joseph. Luke's account is probably the genealogy through Mary via Nathan (v31) or else it could be Joseph's genealogy with one or two levirate marriages showing the birth line rather than the legal line making it slightly different to Matthew's account. Levirate marriages happened when a man died, and his brother married his young widowed wife to raise up seed and provide an inheritance for the family in the land – Deu. 25. 5-6. Either way the genealogies show the real historicity of the birth and life of the Lord Jesus. Luke the historian takes us back to Adam reminding us of how humanity commenced. Unlike Adam, the Lord Jesus exhibited a new form of manhood – perfect, sinless humanity. Adam reflected God: he was made in His image and after His likeness - a son of God (v38). But Adam sinned and became a pale reflection of what he should have been. Now the only-beloved Son of God (v22) had come, who is the 'image of the invisible God' (Col. 1. 15), the full revelation and reflection of God (John 1. 1-2, 18). To see Him was to see everything that God is (John 14. 9). God as a man on earth. Immanuel – God with us (Matt. 1. 23). Luke introduces us to a perfect man.

of Mattathias, which was the son of Semei, which
was the son of Joseph, which was the son of Juda,
27 Which was the son of Joanna, which was the son
of Rhesa, which was the son of Zorobabel, which
was the son of Salathiel, which was the son of Neri,
28 Which was the son of Melchi, which was the son
of Addi, which was the son of Cosam, which was the
son of Elmodam, which was the son of Er,
29 Which was the son of Jose, which was the son of
Eliezer, which was the son of Jorim, which was the
son of Matthat, which was the son of Levi,
30 Which was the son of Simeon, which was the
son of Juda, which was the son of Joseph, which
was the son of Jonan, which was the son of Eliakim,
31 Which was the son of Melea, which was the son
of Menan, which was the son of Mattatha, which
was the son of Nathan, which was the son of David,
32 Which was the son of Jesse, which was the son
of Obed, which was the son of Booz, which was
the son of Salmon, which was the son of Naasson,
33 Which was the son of Aminadab, which was the
son of Aram, which was the son of Esrom, which
was the son of Phares, which was the son of Juda,
34 Which was the son of Jacob, which was the son
of Isaac, which was the son of Abraham, which was
the son of Thara, which was the son of Nachor,
35 Which was the son of Saruch, which was the son
of Ragau, which was the son of Phalec, which was
the son of Heber, which was the son of Sala,
36 Which was the son of Cainan, which was the son
of Arphaxad, which was the son of Sem, which was
the son of Noe, which was the son of Lamech,
37 Which was the son of Mathusala, which was the
son of Enoch, which was the son of Jared, which was
the son of Maleleel, which was the son of Cainan,
38 Which was the son of Enos, which was the son
of Seth, which was the son of Adam, which was the
son of God.

Reflective Questions and Notes

A. Try and summarise what John the Baptist preached? v1-14

B. What did John say about the Lord Jesus? v15-17

C. What did the Father say about the Lord Jesus? v21-22

D. What is the purpose of this genealogy of Christ? v23-38

Luke 4

Chapter 4: The Word of God

4.1 Others had been 'filled' with the Holy Spirit but of no other person was it said that He was 'full of the Holy Spirit'.

4.2 This is the first mention of the devil. He was a fallen angel and is the chief adversary of God. His power was disannulled at the cross of Christ (Hebrews 2. 14-15) and he will one day be placed in the lake of fire (Rev. 20. 10).

4.3 'If' means 'since'. Affirmation not supposition.

4.3-4 The devil said, *'Satisfy yourself'.* This was a test of His *dependency* upon God and *self-indulgence.* Would the Lord Jesus be willing to use His power to meet His own needs? The answer is 'No!'.

4.5-8. The devil said, *'Spare yourself'.* This was a test of His *humility and self-preservation.* The devil is suggesting that He could have the crown without the cross. The Lord Jesus knew that before He could reign in power over the world He must first know the suffering and die for the sin of the world at the cross. Nothing would prevent Him from going to the cross- not even the devil.

4.9-12. The devil said, *'Show yourself'.* This was a test of *vanity and self-glorification.* The devil by quoting the Holy Scriptures shows how dangerous it is when verses are partially quoted and taken out of context. The Lord Jesus, by contrast, moved humbly and obediently according to the will of God.

'dash' (v11) means 'strike'.

4.13 The devil is defeated. Forty days of intensive testing of the Saviour are over and the Lord Jesus displays His perfection and superior power.

4.14-15 The Lord Jesus power

The Temptation in the Wilderness

1 And Jesus being full of the Holy Ghost returned
from Jordan, and was led by the Spirit into the
wilderness,
2 Being forty days tempted of the devil. And in
those days he did eat nothing: and when they were
ended, he afterward hungered.
3 And the devil said unto him, If thou be the Son
of God, command this stone that it be made bread.
4 And Jesus answered him, saying, It is written,
That man shall not live by bread alone, but by every
word of God.
5 And the devil, taking him up into an high
mountain, shewed unto him all the kingdoms of
the world in a moment of time.
6 And the devil said unto him, All this power will I
give thee, and the glory of them: for that is delivered
unto me; and to whomsoever I will I give it.
7 If thou therefore wilt worship me, all shall be
thine.
8 And Jesus answered and said unto him, Get
thee behind me, Satan: for it is written, Thou shalt
worship the Lord thy God, and him only shalt thou
serve.
9 And he brought him to Jerusalem, and set him on
a pinnacle of the temple, and said unto him, If thou
be the Son of God, cast thyself down from hence:
10 For it is written, He shall give his angels charge
over thee, to keep thee:
11 And in their hands they shall bear thee up, lest
at any time thou dash thy foot against a stone.
12 And Jesus answering said unto him, It is said,
Thou shalt not tempt the Lord thy God.
13 And when the devil had ended all the temptation,
he departed from him for a season.

The Ministry at Nazareth

14 And Jesus returned in the power of the Spirit into
Galilee: and there went out a fame of him through
all the region round about.
15 And he taught in their synagogues, being
glorified of all.

16 And he came to Nazareth, where he had been
brought up: and, as his custom was, he went into
the synagogue on the sabbath day, and stood up
for to read.
17 And there was delivered unto him the book of
the prophet Esaias. And when he had opened the
book, he found the place where it was written,
18 The Spirit of the Lord is upon me, because he hath
anointed me to preach the gospel to the poor; he
hath sent me to heal the brokenhearted, to preach
deliverance to the captives, and recovering of sight
to the blind, to set at liberty them that are bruised,
19 To preach the acceptable year of the Lord.
20 And he closed the book, and he gave it again to
the minister, and sat down. And the eyes of all them
that were in the synagogue were fastened on him.
21 And he began to say unto them, This day is this
scripture fulfilled in your ears.
22 And all bare him witness, and wondered at the
gracious words which proceeded out of his mouth.
And they said, Is not this Joseph's son?
23 And he said unto them, Ye will surely say unto
me this proverb, Physician, heal thyself: whatsoever
we have heard done in Capernaum, do also here in
thy country.
24 And he said, Verily I say unto you, No prophet is
accepted in his own country.
25 But I tell you of a truth, many widows were in
Israel in the days of Elias, when the heaven was shut
up three years and six months, when great famine
was throughout all the land;
26 But unto none of them was Elias sent, save unto
Sarepta, a city of Sidon, unto a woman that was a
widow.
27 And many lepers were in Israel in the time
of Eliseus the prophet; and none of them was
cleansed, saving Naaman the Syrian.
28 And all they in the synagogue, when they heard
these things, were filled with wrath,
29 And rose up, and thrust him out of the city, and
led him unto the brow of the hill whereon their city
was built, that they might cast him down headlong.

and work was demonstrable and grew in popularity.

4.16 See 2.51 for Nazareth. His custom was to go the place where the Word of God was read. Those who wished to publicly read the Word of God in the synagogue stood up and continued to read from the scroll in a standing position. He was reading the Word of God to all who had seen Him grow up. It would come with added force.

4.17-18 'the book' – we would call it a scroll today. He opened it at Isaiah chapter 61 verses 1-3 and started to read.

4.19 He stopped half way through a sentence. This was the day of grace, the acceptable year of the Lord for salvation, for all people. But the day would come when He would return in judgment. This is what the next part of the sentence in Isaiah 61.2 is all about – 'the day of vengeance of our God'.

4.20 He had not said anything and yet every eye was upon Him. The eternal living Word of God reading the written word of God was mesmerising.

4.21 What a statement! The Word of God was being fulfilled in front of their eyes.

4.22 'Gracious words' – It was not just what the Saviour said that impressed people but how He spoke.

4.23-24. Unbelief about the claims of Christ resulted in them not receiving Him!

4.25 'Elias' is the transliteration of the name Elijah. Elijah the prophet's teaching and movements are recorded for us from 1 Kings 17 through to 2 Kings 2.

4.26 This is a reference to the widow in 1 Kings 17. 8-24.

4.27 This is a reference to 2 Kings 5 when Naaman is cleansed from his leprosy. Remarkably there are no cases of lepers being cleansed from that time until this point.

4.28 The simple testimony of Holy Scripture caused anger, particularly that it was people outwith Israel (Syrian and Sidon) who were blessed.

4.29-30 Their anger and unbelief were deep and resulted in them seeking to kill the Christ but the hour of His death had been planned from eternity to be on the Passover day as the 'Lamb of God' and so with dignity and power He passed through them all.

4.31-32 He preached at Capernaum which was on the side of the sea of Galilee. People were astounded with the power of His preaching.

4.33 'spirit of an unclean devil' i.e. he was demon possessed.

4.34 Demons know who the Christ of God is – the Holy One of God. They also know that He is opposed to them.

4.35 The word of Christ was sufficient to release this man from the demon.

4.36-37 All were shocked. The miracles of Christ brought about a powerful testimony to the Word of Christ, resulting in a much wider circle hearing of the words and works of Christ.

4.38 Simon is the Apostle Peter. His name was changed from Simon to Peter. Simon's wife mother was severely ill with a raging temperature.

4.39 Not only was she healed but had the strength to look after others. The miracles of Christ were real and verifiable.

4.40 'divers' means 'many'.

That evening was an evening full of healing. Not one was turned away, all that were sick were brought to Him.

4.41 He never permitted lying lips to speak His praise.

30 But he passing through the midst of them went his way,

The Ministry at Capernaum

31 And came down to Capernaum, a city of Galilee, and taught them on the sabbath days.

32 And they were astonished at his doctrine: for his word was with power.

33 And in the synagogue there was a man, which had a spirit of an unclean devil, and cried out with a loud voice,

34 Saying, Let us alone; what have we to do with thee, thou Jesus of Nazareth? art thou come to destroy us? I know thee who thou art; the Holy One of God.

35 And Jesus rebuked him, saying, Hold thy peace, and come out of him. And when the devil had thrown him in the midst, he came out of him, and hurt him not.

36 And they were all amazed, and spake among themselves, saying, What a word is this! for with authority and power he commandeth the unclean spirits, and they come out.

37 And the fame of him went out into every place of the country round about.

The Healing of Peter's Wife's Mother

38 And he arose out of the synagogue, and entered into Simon's house. And Simon's wife's mother was taken with a great fever; and they besought him for her.

39 And he stood over her, and rebuked the fever; and it left her: and immediately she arose and ministered unto them.

40 Now when the sun was setting, all they that had any sick with divers diseases brought them unto him; and he laid his hands on every one of them, and healed them.

41 And devils also came out of many, crying out, and saying, Thou art Christ the Son of God. And he rebuking them suffered them not to speak: for they knew that he was Christ.

42 And when it was day, he departed and went into a desert place: and the people sought him, and

came unto him, and stayed him, that he should not
depart from them.
43 And he said unto them, I must preach the
kingdom of God to other cities also: for therefore
am I sent.
44 And he preached in the synagogues of Galilee.

4.42 'stayed him' means 'restrained him'. They did not want Him to leave!

4.43 The Lord had taught them the truth of the gospel and they now had a responsibility to believe it by faith. Other places now had to hear the message too. 'The kingdom of God' - God is a king and has a kingdom. Is He your king? Are you one of His subjects? There is a spiritual kingdom that is growing and will soon be complete with a people that acknowledge that Christ is Lord. There will also be a literal kingdom one day upon earth when Christ returns and where Christ will reign.

Reflective Questions and Notes

A. What were the big tests the devil set the Christ of God? Are these tests still relevant to us? v1-13

B. What did the Lord read in Nazareth and what was His message? Was it accepted? v14-30

C. Where did the power lie for the Lord to do miracles and save people? v30-39

D. Why was the Lord Jesus sent into the world? v43-44

____

____

____

____

____

Luke 5

The Miracle of the Great Number of Fish

1 And it came to pass, that, as the people pressed
upon him to hear the word of God, he stood by the
lake of Gennesaret,
2 And saw two ships standing by the lake: but
the fishermen were gone out of them, and were
washing their nets.
3 And he entered into one of the ships, which was
Simon's, and prayed him that he would thrust out
a little from the land. And he sat down, and taught
the people out of the ship.
4 Now when he had left speaking, he said unto
Simon, Launch out into the deep, and let down your
nets for a draught.
5 And Simon answering said unto him, Master, we
have toiled all the night, and have taken nothing:
nevertheless at thy word I will let down the net.
6 And when they had this done, they inclosed a
great multitude of fishes: and their net brake.
7 And they beckoned unto their partners, which
were in the other ship, that they should come and
help them. And they came, and filled both the ships,
so that they began to sink.
8 When Simon Peter saw it, he fell down at Jesus'
knees, saying, Depart from me; for I am a sinful
man, O Lord.
9 For he was astonished, and all that were with him,
at the draught of the fishes which they had taken:
10 And so was also James, and John, the sons of
Zebedee, which were partners with Simon. And
Jesus said unto Simon, Fear not; from henceforth
thou shalt catch men.
11 And when they had brought their ships to land,
they forsook all, and followed him.

The Healing of a Leper

12 And it came to pass, when he was in a certain
city, behold a man full of leprosy: who seeing Jesus
fell on his face, and besought him, saying, Lord, if
thou wilt, thou canst make me clean.
13 And he put forth his hand, and touched him,

Chapter 5: Sin and cleansing.

5.1 Lake Gennesaret is normally called the Sea of Galilee or Lake Tiberias. It is a freshwater lake in Israel around 21 km long.

5.2 Fishermen washing nets at the side of the lake would be a familiar sight.

5.3 The Lord Jesus used the boat as a platform. The Rabbis sat to teach. The Saviour by choosing to sit down and preach was indicating that what He had to say was authoritative and important.

5.4 'draught' means a net full of fish.

5.5-6 Simon Peter acknowledges his previous futile efforts to catch anything feeling his utter emptiness and weakness but at the word of Christ, despite reluctance, he does drop the net into the sea. And when he does this the net is so full of fish that it breaks.

5.7 Their partners were James and John (v10) Both ships are now full of fish and sinking!

5.8 Peter realises that he had committed the biggest sin of all – the sin of unbelief - he falls at the knees of Christ repenting of sin and calling Him Lord.

5.9 They were astounded at One who had authority over creation to direct a shoal of fish into their net. He was Lord of creation.

5.10 Simon is being called away from being a fishermen to be being a fisher (catcher) of men. God's salvation brings a new purpose to life.

5.11 These men Peter, James and John (and Andrew, Mark 1. 16-18) left their boats, their amazing shoal of fish to others and lived entirely by faith in the service of Christ. They followed Him.

5.12 'Lord' – the man takes the place of a servant and

acknowledges the complete authority of Christ.
'if thou wilt' – if You are willing. 'You can make me clean' – what faith in His power (see 4.27)!
5.13 'I will' – The Saviour not only had the power, but He had the willingness to heal.
5.14 The priest would never have seen a leper cleansed. He would have read Leviticus 14 but never had to put it into practice. Now he would see a demonstration of the power of Christ.
5.16 Christ praying is a theme in Luke's Gospel (3. 21; 9. 18, 29; 11. 1; 22.32, 41, 44)
5.17 – 'doctors of the law' – recognised experts in the Jewish Scriptures. 'power of the Lord was present to heal them' – spiritual healing was available for all, but it appears that only one man accepted it.
5.18 'palsy' means paralysed. 'sought means' – means 'seeking ways to bring their friend to Christ'
5.19 'couch' – means 'bed/mat'.
5.20 What incredible words – The salvation of Christ means sins are all forgiven immediately and personally.
5.21 The religious community were not happy at this man's conversion. What they said was right, only God can forgive sin, but they did not realise that Jesus was God as a man on earth.
5.22 The Lord Jesus reads minds.
5.23 They might think it was much easier to say 'your sins are forgiven' than make the man walk. A word from the Saviour would heal the man. For sins to be forgiven it required a sacrifice for sin and involved Christ going to the cross to die for this man's sins.
5.24 What a claim! He has the power to forgive sins and demonstrated that power.
5.25-26 This miracle was not done

saying, I will: be thou clean. And immediately the leprosy departed from him.

14 And he charged him to tell no man: but go, and shew thyself to the priest, and offer for thy cleansing, according as Moses commanded, for a testimony unto them.

15 But so much the more went there a fame abroad of him: and great multitudes came together to hear, and to be healed by him of their infirmities.

16 And he withdrew himself into the wilderness, and prayed.

The Miracle of a Paralytic

17 And it came to pass on a certain day, as he was teaching, that there were Pharisees and doctors of the law sitting by, which were come out of every town of Galilee, and Judaea, and Jerusalem: and the power of the Lord was present to heal them.

18 And, behold, men brought in a bed a man which was taken with a palsy: and they sought means to bring him in, and to lay him before him.

19 And when they could not find by what way they might bring him in because of the multitude, they went upon the housetop, and let him down through the tiling with his couch into the midst before Jesus.

20 And when he saw their faith, he said unto him, Man, thy sins are forgiven thee.

21 And the scribes and the Pharisees began to reason, saying, Who is this which speaketh blasphemies? Who can forgive sins, but God alone?

22 But when Jesus perceived their thoughts, he answering said unto them, What reason ye in your hearts?

23 Whether is easier, to say, Thy sins be forgiven thee; or to say, Rise up and walk?

24 **But that ye may know that the Son of man hath power upon earth to forgive sins**, (he said unto the sick of the palsy,) I say unto thee, Arise, and take up thy couch, and go into thine house.

25 And immediately he rose up before them, and took up that whereon he lay, and departed to his own house, glorifying God.

26 And they were all amazed, and they glorified

God, and were filled with fear, saying, We have seen
strange things to day.

The Call of Matthew

27 And after these things he went forth, and saw
a publican, named Levi, sitting at the receipt of
custom: and he said unto him, Follow me.
28 And he left all, rose up, and followed him.
29 And Levi made him a great feast in his own house:
and there was a great company of publicans and of
others that sat down with them.
30 But their scribes and Pharisees murmured against
his disciples, saying, Why do ye eat and drink with
publicans and sinners?
31 And Jesus answering said unto them, They that
are whole need not a physician; but they that are
sick.
32 **I came not to call the righteous, but sinners
to repentance**.

Fasting and Things New and Old

33 And they said unto him, Why do the disciples of
John fast often, and make prayers, and likewise the
disciples of the Pharisees; but thine eat and drink?
34 And he said unto them, Can ye make the children
of the bridechamber fast, while the bridegroom is
with them?
35 But the days will come, when the bridegroom
shall be taken away from them, and then shall they
fast in those days.
36 And he spake also a parable unto them; No man
putteth a piece of a new garment upon an old; if
otherwise, then both the new maketh a rent, and
the piece that was taken out of the new agreeth
not with the old.
37 And no man putteth new wine into old bottles;
else the new wine will burst the bottles, and be
spilled, and the bottles shall perish.
38 But new wine must be put into new bottles; and
both are preserved.
39 No man also having drunk old wine straightway
desireth new: for he saith, The old is better.

in a private way. This miracle brought about public worship and a reverential fear and awe.

5.27-28 Levi the publican (tax collector) is also called Matthew and he responds immediately to the call of Christ

5.29-30 There are always those (particularly religious people like the Pharisees) who think that they are more 'holy' than most people and despise others. Romans 3. 22-23 says 'there is no difference... for all have sinned'.

5.31-32 The Lord Jesus claimed to be the Great Doctor (meaning of the word Physician) who had come to heal the sickness of sin in humanity. Unfortunately, there were some who thought they had 'no need' of the Great Doctor.

5.33-35 Some felt that salvation was to be found in denying the body's desire for food (fasting) and other religious rituals. The Lord Jesus said that salvation was joy in a person, just like the joy the wedding guests have when they see the Bridegroom. He said He was like the Bridegroom and that one day He would have to leave them. He was referring to His ascension back to the Father.

5.36-39 Trying to sew a new patch of cloth on an old threadbare garment results in the hole getting worse ('a rent') and it does not fit with the old cloth. We need new clothes. The Lord Jesus was saying that salvation is not a 'patch-up job' on our sins, but a new life altogether. We need to turn from our old life of sin and accept new life in Christ. New wine in old wine skins causes a chemical reaction and allows the wine to leak out. We need new life in Christ not a 'make over'. The problem is people are reluctant to give up the old way of life saying the 'old is better'.

Reflective Questions and Notes

A. What was Peter's sin? v8

B. What was the leper's request and what was the answer of the Lord? v12-13

C. What did the paralysed man receive and from whom? v20-26

D. Why did the Lord Jesus come? v31-32

Luke 6

Lord of the Sabbath

1 And it came to pass on the second sabbath after
the first, that he went through the corn fields; and
his disciples plucked the ears of corn, and did eat,
rubbing them in their hands.
2 And certain of the Pharisees said unto them, Why
do ye that which is not lawful to do on the sabbath
days?
3 And Jesus answering them said, Have ye not read
so much as this, what David did, when himself was
an hungred, and they which were with him;
4 How he went into the house of God, and did take
and eat the shewbread, and gave also to them that
were with him; which it is not lawful to eat but for
the priests alone?
5 And he said unto them, That the Son of man is
Lord also of the sabbath.
6 And it came to pass also on another sabbath, that
he entered into the synagogue and taught: and
there was a man whose right hand was withered.
7 And the scribes and Pharisees watched him,
whether he would heal on the sabbath day; that
they might find an accusation against him.
8 But he knew their thoughts, and said to the man
which had the withered hand, Rise up, and stand
forth in the midst. And he arose and stood forth.
9 Then said Jesus unto them, I will ask you one thing;
Is it lawful on the sabbath days to do good, or to do
evil? to save life, or to destroy it?
10 And looking round about upon them all, he said
unto the man, Stretch forth thy hand. And he did
so: and his hand was restored whole as the other.
11 And they were filled with madness; and
communed one with another what they might do
to Jesus.

The Calling of the Twelve

12 And it came to pass in those days, that he went
out into a mountain to pray, and continued all night
in prayer to God.
13 And when it was day, he called unto him his

Chapter 6: Hypocrisy

6.1 The first sabbath would be at the Passover and start of the feast of Unleavened Bread. The second sabbath would be at the end of the seven-day feast of Unleavened Bread. Around March/April time.

6.2 Religious legalism even meant that a new human rule had been brought in that you could not rub corn in your hand on the Sabbath day.

6.3-5 The Lord answers their religious reasoning by Scripture, reminding them that when David was very hungry he actually ate of the loaves in the Holy Place in the day when Saul was going to kill him (I Sam 20. 1-6). God will always allow us to meet need whatever the circumstances. He said that it was He as Son of Man who had created the sabbath (what a claim!). It was to be an opportunity for people to rest not for man-made rules which keep people oppressed!

6.6-10 The Lord then demonstrates His teaching against religious legalism by healing the man with the withered (v6- shrivelled) hand by healing him so publicly on the sabbath day in the synagogue. The Lord never half completed a job– his hand was restored to the same use as the other one!

6.11 People say seeing is believing. It is not true. Even seeing miracles cannot save people.

6.12 – See note on 5.16. In 5.16 it is the isolation of prayer ('withdrew into the wilderness') that is in view, here it is the elevation of prayer ('into a mountain') and the persistency of prayer ('continued all night').

6.13-16 He chose. It was His

decision who the apostles would be. Fishermen like Peter and John, tax collectors like Matthew, politicians like Simon the zealot. What a disparate group of people and yet he bound them together as one band for His glory. He chose twelve! He chose Judas Iscariot. He knew he would be the traitor before Judas did. He had a purpose in choosing Judas, it was all part of God's plan to redeem the human race. He did not choose Judas so that he could sin.
6.17-19 Tyre and Zidon this is in present day Lebanon. Large crowds came from large distances to hear the Christ and to see Him heal people who were demon possessed and sick. His healing power was available to all.
6.20-23 The Lord's four beatitudes in Luke's Gospel (See Matthew 5.1-12 for a fuller list) are worth meditating upon. The word blessed literally means 'happy'. He taught that true happiness is found in poverty, hunger, weeping and hatred! These counter-intuitive thoughts are explained in Mathew's Gospel. He is saying that when I see that this world is nothing but a pauper then I will know the riches of the Kingdom of God. When I hunger for the Word of God then I will be filled. When I weep for Christ and for the spiritual conditions in the land then I will know true laughter, when I experience persecution for Christ that is when I can rejoice knowing that anything done for His sake will be rewarded eternally in heaven.
6.24-26 The four blessings are followed by four woes. Woes to the rich, self-satisfied ('full'), laughing, and lauded stands in contrast to the poor, hungry, weeping and despised. It really is a description of those living for this world. All that they have and

disciples: and of them he chose twelve, whom also
he named apostles;
14 Simon, (whom he also named Peter,) and
Andrew his brother, James and John, Philip and
Bartholomew,
15 Matthew and Thomas, James the son of Alphaeus,
and Simon called Zelotes,
16 And Judas the brother of James, and Judas
Iscariot, which also was the traitor.

The Lord's Instruction to His Disciples

17 And he came down with them, and stood in the
plain, and the company of his disciples, and a great
multitude of people out of all Judaea and Jerusalem,
and from the sea coast of Tyre and Sidon, which
came to hear him, and to be healed of their diseases;
18 And they that were vexed with unclean spirits:
and they were healed.
19 And the whole multitude sought to touch him:
for there went virtue out of him, and healed them
all.
20 And he lifted up his eyes on his disciples, and
said, Blessed be ye poor: for yours is the kingdom
of God.
21 Blessed are ye that hunger now: for ye shall be
filled. Blessed are ye that weep now: for ye shall
laugh.
22 Blessed are ye, when men shall hate you, and
when they shall separate you from their company,
and shall reproach you, and cast out your name as
evil, for the Son of man's sake.
23 Rejoice ye in that day, and leap for joy: for,
behold, your reward is great in heaven: for in the
like manner did their fathers unto the prophets.
24 But woe unto you that are rich! for ye have
received your consolation.
25 Woe unto you that are full! for ye shall hunger.
Woe unto you that laugh now! for ye shall mourn
and weep.
26 Woe unto you, when all men shall speak well of
you! for so did their fathers to the false prophets.
27 But I say unto you which hear, Love your enemies,
do good to them which hate you,

28 Bless them that curse you, and pray for them which despitefully use you.
29 And unto him that smiteth thee on the one cheek offer also the other; and him that taketh away thy cloak forbid not to take thy coat also.
30 Give to every man that asketh of thee; and of him that taketh away thy goods ask them not again.
31 And as ye would that men should do to you, do ye also to them likewise.
32 For if ye love them which love you, what thank have ye? for sinners also love those that love them.
33 And if ye do good to them which do good to you, what thank have ye? for sinners also do even the same.
34 And if ye lend to them of whom ye hope to receive, what thank have ye? for sinners also lend to sinners, to receive as much again.
35 But love ye your enemies, and do good, and lend, hoping for nothing again; and your reward shall be great, and ye shall be the children of the Highest: for he is kind unto the unthankful and to the evil.
36 Be ye therefore merciful, as your Father also is merciful.
37 Judge not, and ye shall not be judged: condemn not, and ye shall not be condemned: forgive, and ye shall be forgiven:
38 Give, and it shall be given unto you; good measure, pressed down, and shaken together, and running over, shall men give into your bosom. For with the same measure that ye mete withal it shall be measured to you again.
39 And he spake a parable unto them, Can the blind lead the blind? shall they not both fall into the ditch?
40 The disciple is not above his master: but every one that is perfect shall be as his master.
41 And why beholdest thou the mote that is in thy brother's eye, but perceivest not the beam that is in thine own eye?
42 Either how canst thou say to thy brother, Brother, let me pull out the mote that is in thine eye, when thou thyself beholdest not the beam that is in thine

ever have is for this world. It ends in disaster.

6.27-31 After the four blessings and four woes comes four injunctions. Love (v27), Bless (v28), Offer (v29), and Give (v30) with the golden rule of v31 summarising these four actions. The Lord's teaching is high ground – love your enemies and not just in a theoretical way – 'do good to them'. Bless (give thanks) and pray for those that curse you. Offer more to those that wrong you. Give to those that take from you. Live towards others as you would wish others live towards you. We can only live this way by the strengthening power of Christ.

6.32-35 There are now three 'ifs' explaining the four injunctions and ending with a great exhortation (v35). The first 'if' is the 'if' of love – believers need to be able to love those that do not love them back. The second 'if' is the 'if' of goodness- believers need to be able to be good to those who do not return the favour. The third 'if' is the 'if' of lending- believers need to be able to lend support to others and never receive anything back. These are the actions that will show the world that a true believer in Christ is different. These conditions are brought together in v35 and show that God's people will be blessed eternally for exhibiting them, as they are a reflection of the character of the true God.

6.36 -37 Four graces are to be seen. Two positive – mercy and forgiveness. Two negative – do not judge or condemn (instead forbear and give thanks).

6.38 The final request is to give liberally, and concentrated, super-abundant goodness, will be passed back to you. How we give is how we will receive.

6.39-42 The Lord's teaching now turns back to hypocrisy. Hypocritical leaders are blind and if we allow them to lead us then we will fall (v40). We should seek to emulate our leaders but not false ones – Christ is the ultimate One we must follow (v41). Watch out for the hypocritical eye. The Lord uses hyperbole to make the point so forcibly (v42)!
6.43-44 The metaphor for hypocrisy now changes from our eye to trees and fruit. True authenticity is seen in fruit in the life. Hypocrisy can be spotted in the fruit in people's lives – just as figs are not found on thorn bushes so the graces of Christ are not found on angry rude, worldly and proud people.
6.45-47 What comes out of the mouth tells us all about the heart. If people say 'Lord, Lord' but their life is a denial of it then they are false. But those that show in their lives that they are obedient to Christ's words are true.
6.48-49 The illustration of the true authentic disciple of Christ and the hypocritical false disciple is illustrated in two houses. Both looked the same but had entirely different foundations. It was only when the storms came that the house built on sandy earth fell down and collapsed but the one built on the rock was unaffected. (another title for Christ 1 Cor 10.4). The day of judgment is coming and it will expose all hypocrisy. On which foundation are you building?

own eye? Thou hypocrite, cast out first the beam out of thine own eye, and then shalt thou see clearly to pull out the mote that is in thy brother's eye.
43 For a good tree bringeth not forth corrupt fruit; neither doth a corrupt tree bring forth good fruit.
44 For every tree is known by his own fruit. For of thorns men do not gather figs, nor of a bramble bush gather they grapes.
45 A good man out of the good treasure of his heart bringeth forth that which is good; and an evil man out of the evil treasure of his heart bringeth forth that which is evil: for of the abundance of the heart his mouth speaketh.
46 And why call ye me, Lord, Lord, and do not the things which I say?
47 Whosoever cometh to me, and heareth my sayings, and doeth them, I will shew you to whom he is like:
48 He is like a man which built an house, and digged deep, and laid the foundation on a rock: and when the flood arose, the stream beat vehemently upon that house, and could not shake it: for it was founded upon a rock.
49 But he that heareth, and doeth not, is like a man that without a foundation built an house upon the earth; against which the stream did beat vehemently, and immediately it fell; and the ruin of that house was great.

Reflective Questions and Notes

A. What Old Testament example did the Lord use to expose the religious rule making by the Pharisees? What claim did He make? v3-4, v5-11

B. What were the Lord's four blessings, and four woes? v20-26

C. What were the Lord's four injunctions and three 'ifs'? v27-35

D. What did the Lord say about the hypocrite's eyes, heart, mouth and houses? v39-49

Luke 7

The Centurion's Servant Healed

1 Now when he had ended all his sayings in the
audience of the people, he entered into Capernaum.
2 And a certain centurion's servant, who was dear
unto him, was sick, and ready to die.
3 And when he heard of Jesus, he sent unto him the
elders of the Jews, beseeching him that he would
come and heal his servant.
4 And when they came to Jesus, they besought him
instantly, saying, That he was worthy for whom he
should do this:
5 For he loveth our nation, and he hath built us a
synagogue.
6 Then Jesus went with them. And when he was
now not far from the house, the centurion sent
friends to him, saying unto him, Lord, trouble not
thyself: for I am not worthy that thou shouldest
enter under my roof:
7 Wherefore neither thought I myself worthy to
come unto thee: but say in a word, and my servant
shall be healed.
8 For I also am a man set under authority, having
under me soldiers, and I say unto one, Go, and he
goeth; and to another, Come, and he cometh; and
to my servant, Do this, and he doeth it.
9 When Jesus heard these things, he marvelled
at him, and turned him about, and said unto the
people that followed him, I say unto you, I have not
found so great faith, no, not in Israel.
10 And they that were sent, returning to the house,
found the servant whole that had been sick.

The Raising of a Widow's Son

11 And it came to pass the day after, that he went
into a city called Nain; and many of his disciples
went with him, and much people.
12 Now when he came nigh to the gate of he city,
behold, there was a dead man carried out, the only
son of his mother, and she was a widow: and much
people of the city was with her.
13 And when the Lord saw her, he had compassion
on her, and said unto her, Weep not.

Chapter 7: Faith

7.1 Capernaum –by Lake Galilee where the Lord often stayed. Roman guard stationed here.

7.2-10 The greatest faith in Israel was not shown by a Jew but a Gentile (v9) – a Roman centurion. His concern for his servant shows his compassion (v2-3). The attitude of the people is illuminating. They believed that our good words and charitable acts should merit the blessing of God (v4-5), although God says the opposite (Eph. 2. 8). What pride! However, the Centurion himself does not believe that he is worthy to have the Lord in his house (v6). What humility and reverence. He also has outstanding faith believing that the Lord Jesus' word carries power across the boundaries of time and space (v7-8) although he had never seen the Lord perform a miracle. When the Centurion went home his servant was well again.

7.11-13 The next miracle recorded is outside Nain, a city in Galilee, standing on the north-western slope of the "hill Moreh", about 25 miles from Capernaum. Before Nain stands the great plain of Esdraelon. A lady had lost her husband and now has lost her only son. Families of only one son or girl are a theme in Luke's Gospel (8. 42; 9. 38). This miracle is not so much an impossible distance (as with the Centurion's servant) but an impossible moment and time. The funeral was already happening. When the Lord saw the funeral procession, He had compassion on the lady and told her to dry up her tears.

7.14-17 The Lord interrupts the funeral procession and touched the stand on which the body

14 And he came and touched the bier: and they that bare him stood still. And he said, Young man, I say unto thee, Arise.
15 And he that was dead sat up, and began to speak. And he delivered him to his mother.
16 And there came a fear on all: and they glorified God, saying, That a great prophet is risen up among us; and, That God hath visited his people.
17 And this rumour of him went forth throughout all Judaea, and throughout all the region round about.

The Question of John the Baptist

18 And the disciples of John shewed him of all these things.
19 And John calling unto him two of his disciples sent them to Jesus, saying, Art thou he that should come? or look we for another?
20 When the men were come unto him, they said, John Baptist hath sent us unto thee, saying, Art thou he that should come? or look we for another?
21 And in that same hour he cured many of their infirmities and plagues, and of evil spirits; and unto many that were blind he gave sight.
22 Then Jesus answering said unto them, Go your way, and tell John what things ye have seen and heard; how that the blind see, the lame walk, the lepers are cleansed, the deaf hear, the dead are raised, to the poor the gospel is preached.
23 And blessed is he, whosoever shall not be offended in me.
24 And when the messengers of John were departed, he began to speak unto the people concerning John, What went ye out into the wilderness for to see? A reed shaken with the wind?
25 But what went ye out for to see? A man clothed in soft raiment? Behold, they which are gorgeously apparelled, and live delicately, are in kings' courts.
26 But what went ye out for to see? A prophet? Yea, I say unto you, and much more than a prophet.
27 This is he, of whom it is written, Behold, I send my messenger before thy face, which shall prepare thy way before thee.
28 For I say unto you, Among those that are born

had been placed ('bier' v14) and speaks to the corpse directly. The young man sits up and gives evidence of the life he now has. He is delivered back to his mother (v15). What a lovely touch. The response is one of reverential awe and worship. There was no doubt that God had spoken directly and publicly and this spread throughout the land (v16-17).

7.18-23 **The Lord's testimony to John the Baptist.** John's disciples had heard of the healing of the Centurion's servant and the raising of the young man in Nain. John in his weakness and isolation sends from the Herod's prison cell to have affirmed to him once more the Saviour's claim to Messiahship. The very message he had preached and that had resulted in him being imprisoned and ultimately killed. The Lord answers by actions (His miracles) and not words (v21-22)! His encouragement to John was that the prophet's words in Isaiah 61.1-3 were being unfolded in front of everyone's eyes. The Scriptures were to be John's comfort and blessing in his last days on earth.

7.24-28. **The Lord's testimony of John the Baptist.** The Lord Jesus speaks of John the Baptist in the highest possible terms – stable and dependable (v24); humble and unmaterialistic (v25). John spoke for God (v26) and he was written of in the Word of God hundreds of years before his birth (Isaiah 40. 1-4) that he would prepare the way for the Christ (v27). He was the greatest prophet ever born with the obvious exception of the Lord (v28).

7.29-30 **The response to the Lord's praise of John the Baptist.** The crowd was pleased as they had believed John and repented of their sin, were baptised and looked for the Messiah. The religious Pharisees were the complete opposite: they rejected John's counsel and did not get baptised. This is a reminder that religion can blind us to blessing from God.

7.30-35 The Lord likens the religious pharisees to little children with instruments at the market square who are always wanting feedback on everything that they do and changing their tune depending on the audience in order to get more out of people (v32). John had been a pilgrim and teetotal and they called him a demon (v33). The Lord had eaten and drunk with them and they called Him a glutton (v34). They were spiritually immature and unstable. Winebibber (v34) means to consume a lot of wine. Our Lord did not do that!

7.36- 50. The House of Simon the Pharisee. It was in this house that the proud Pharisee Simon was taught a lesson. A lady arrived into the first part of the house (which was traditionally open in the East). She brings extremely expensive perfume and poured it on the feet of Christ, mingling it with her tears and wiping them with her hair. Simon immediately judges Christ and the women but keeps his facial profile the same. He reckons the woman is a sinner and below him.

7.41-42 The Lord tells him a story of two men who were both in debt. One by a large amount and the other by a little amount. Both had their debts removed by the creditor (the man who was owed the money).

7.42-43 The Lord asks Simon who will love the creditor the most and Simon replies that it is the person that is forgiven the most.

7.44-50 The Lord points to the

of women there is not a greater prophet than John the Baptist: but he that is least in the kingdom of God is greater than he.

29 And all the people that heard him, and the publicans, justified God, being baptized with the baptism of John.

30 But the Pharisees and lawyers rejected the counsel of God against themselves, being not baptized of him.

31 And the Lord said, Whereunto then shall I liken the men of this generation? and to what are they like?

32 They are like unto children sitting in the marketplace, and calling one to another, and saying, We have piped unto you, and ye have not danced; we have mourned to you, and ye have not wept.

33 For John the Baptist came neither eating bread nor drinking wine; and ye say, He hath a devil.

34 The Son of man is come eating and drinking; and ye say, Behold a gluttonous man, and a winebibber, a friend of publicans and sinners!

35 But wisdom is justified of all her children.

The Forgiveness and Gratitude of a True Believer

36 And one of the Pharisees desired him that he would eat with him. And he went into the Pharisee's house, and sat down to meat.

37 And, behold, a woman in the city, which was a sinner, when she knew that Jesus sat at meat in the Pharisee's house, brought an alabaster box of ointment,

38 And stood at his feet behind him weeping, and began to wash his feet with tears, and did wipe them with the hairs of her head, and kissed his feet, and anointed them with the ointment.

39 Now when the Pharisee which had bidden him saw it, he spake within himself, saying, This man, if he were a prophet, would have known who and what manner of woman this is that toucheth him: for she is a sinner.

40 And Jesus answering said unto him, Simon, I have somewhat to say unto thee. And he saith, Master, say on.

41 There was a certain creditor which had two
debtors: the one owed five hundred pence, and
the other fifty.
42 And when they had nothing to pay, he frankly
forgave them both. Tell me therefore, which of them
will love him most?
43 Simon answered and said, I suppose that he, to
whom he forgave most. And he said unto him, Thou
hast rightly judged.
44 And he turned to the woman, and said unto
Simon, Seest thou this woman? I entered into thine
house, thou gavest me no water for my feet: but she
hath washed my feet with tears, and wiped them
with the hairs of her head.
45 Thou gavest me no kiss: but this woman since
the time I came in hath not ceased to kiss my feet.
46 My head with oil thou didst not anoint: but this
woman hath anointed my feet with ointment.
47 Wherefore I say unto thee, Her sins, which are
many, are forgiven; for she loved much: but to whom
little is forgiven, the same loveth little.
48 And he said unto her, Thy sins are forgiven.
49 And they that sat at meat with him began to
say within themselves, Who is this that forgiveth
sins also?
50 And he said to the woman, **Thy faith hath saved
thee; go in peace**.

women and indicates that this women loved Him more than he did because she believed that the Lord had forgiven all her sin (v47). Simon never gave the Lord the common eastern greeting of a kiss (v45), but she had. Simon had not offered the common eastern courtesy of having your sandals removed and feet washed, but she had (v44). She loved the Lord. The Lord warned Simon 'if you do not think you need forgiveness you will never love Me'. He turned to the women saying 'your sins are forgiven you' (v48). And when the religious people wondered how He had the authority to say this (v49), He spoke again to the lady saying, 'you are saved by faith (Eph . 2.8) now go on and enjoy My peace (v50)'.

This important episode in Luke reminds us that religion cannot grant forgiveness, indeed it can blind us to it. Pride can rob us of eternal blessing. It reminds us, no matter who we are that the Lord Jesus loves us unconditionally. It also reminds us that we can be forgiven all our sins by Christ and those who are saved, love Christ and no task will be too big or too small to do for Him.

Reflective Questions and Notes

A. Who has the greatest faith in Israel? Why? v9

B. What strengthened John the Baptist's faith at the end of his life? v18-23

C. Who was the greatest prophet ever born? What was his role? v24-30

D. What was it that saved the soul of the lady who came into Simon's house? What did she receive from the Lord? v50, v48

Luke 8

Journeys Throughout Galilee

1 And it came to pass afterward, that he went
throughout every city and village, preaching and
shewing the glad tidings of the kingdom of God:
and the twelve were with him,
2 And certain women, which had been healed of
evil spirits and infirmities, Mary called Magdalene,
out of whom went seven devils,
3 And Joanna the wife of Chuza Herod's steward,
and Susanna, and many others, which ministered
unto him of their substance.

The Parable of the Sower

4 And when much people were gathered together,
and were come to him out of every city, he spake
by a parable:
5 A sower went out to sow his seed: and as he sowed,
some fell by the way side; and it was trodden down,
and the fowls of the air devoured it.
6 And some fell upon a rock; and as soon as it was
sprung up, it withered away, because it lacked
moisture.
7 And some fell among thorns; and the thorns
sprang up with it, and choked it.
8 And other fell on good ground, and sprang up,
and bare fruit an hundredfold. And when he had
said these things, he cried, He that hath ears to
hear, let him hear.
9 And his disciples asked him, saying, What might
this parable be?
10 And he said, Unto you it is given to know the
mysteries of the kingdom of God: but to others
in parables; that seeing they might not see, and
hearing they might not understand.
11 Now the parable is this: The seed is the word
of God.
12 Those by the way side are they that hear; then
cometh the devil, and taketh away the word out of
their hearts, lest they should believe and be saved.
13 They on the rock are they, which, when they
hear, receive the word with joy; and these have

8.1-8.21: Features of the preaching of the Word of God

8.1 The method the Lord used for getting His message across was preaching. The 'twelve' were taught this approach was God's way.

8.2-3 There were some outstanding cases of people's lives being transformed, confirming the power of the Word of God – for example, Mary Magdalene (v2) and Joanna (v3) whose husband was steward to the man that beheaded John the Baptist!

8.4 The Lord often told parables to illustrate spiritual truth.

8.5-15 This parable speaks of a sower sowing seed (v5). We are told that the seed is the Word of God (v11). Some of the seed lands on the path around the field and is soon tramped down or eaten by the birds (v5). This is a picture of the **disinterested hearer (v12)** who has no time for God's Word and treats it with contempt or as soon as God's Word is heard the devil takes any thoughts of eternity away 'lest they should believe and be saved'. How solemn. The next picture is of the seed landing on rocky soil (v6), initially the plant springs up but because there is no depth of soil, the plant cannot root so it dies (v13). This is a picture of the **disillusioned hearer** who initially is attracted to the gospel message but never gets the root of the matter, never repents of sin and so never experiences eternal life. Perhaps this hearer thinks they have 'tried Christianity but it did not work'. The seed also lands on thorny soil (v7,14). But as soon as it lands the thorns block out the sunlight and it is choked to death. This is a picture of the

distracted hearer. The riches and pleasures of this life and its cares and sorrows choke out any spiritual thoughts. The Lord also taught the seed hit good ground. This is the **determined hearer** who hears the Word of God and receives salvation and brings fruit in their life to prove it. All hearers of God's Word must ask which type of soil represents their position in relation to the Word of God?

8.16-18 The Word of God must be sown in order to germinate, must be lit like a lamp in a visible place in order to be seen.

The Word is critical to how we will be used by God. Christians must listen to the Word of God, obey it, and use their gift and opportunities to give the Word of God to others – or lose the opportunity and even the gift to preach.

8.19-21 The Word of God leads to new relationships. Relationships that are even stronger than natural relationships. When we receive the Word of God we become born again (John 3.7) and we are now part of a new spiritual family with spiritual brothers and sisters in Christ. This family is marked by obedience to the Word of God (v21).

8.22-56 Fears and the power of His Word

8.22-26. He said 'Let us go over unto the other side' (v22) and 'they arrived' at the other side (v26). It was never in doubt but in the middle was a great storm and the disciples did doubt(v24)! They were afraid they were going to die. He turned the storm into stillness. They began to worship a man that could control wind and waves, learning that He is God and

no root, which for a while believe, and in time of
temptation fall away.
14 And that which fell among thorns are they, which,
when they have heard, go forth, and are choked with
cares and riches and pleasures of this life, and bring
no fruit to perfection.
15 But that on the good ground are they, which in
an honest and good heart, having heard the word,
keep it, and bring forth fruit with patience.

The Parable of the Lamp

16 No man, when he hath lighted a candle, covereth
it with a vessel, or putteth it under a bed; but setteth
it on a candlestick, that they which enter in may
see the light.
17 For nothing is secret, that shall not be made
manifest; neither any thing hid, that shall not be
known and come abroad.
18 Take heed therefore how ye hear: for whosoever
hath, to him shall be given; and whosoever hath
not, from him shall be taken even that which he
seemeth to have.

Natural and Spiritual Relationships

19 Then came to him his mother and his brethren,
and could not come at him for the press.
20 And it was told him by certain which said, Thy
mother and thy brethren stand without, desiring
to see thee.
21 And he answered and said unto them, My mother
and my brethren are these which hear the word of
God, and do it.

The Miracle of the Storm Calmed

22 Now it came to pass on a certain day, that he
went into a ship with his disciples: and he said unto
them, Let us go over unto the other side of the lake.
And they launched forth.
23 But as they sailed he fell asleep: and there came
down a storm of wind on the lake; and they were
filled with water, and were in jeopardy.
24 And they came to him, and awoke him, saying,
Master, master, we perish. Then he arose, and
rebuked the wind and the raging of the water: and
they ceased, and there was a calm.

25 And he said unto them, Where is your faith? And they being afraid wondered, saying one to another, What manner of man is this! for he commandeth even the winds and water, and they obey him.

The Demon-Possessed Man of Gadara Healed

26 And they arrived at the country of the Gadarenes, which is over against Galilee.
27 And when he went forth to land, there met him out of the city a certain man, which had devils long time, and ware no clothes, neither abode in any house, but in the tombs.
28 When he saw Jesus, he cried out, and fell down before him, and with a loud voice said, What have I to do with thee, Jesus, thou Son of God most high? I beseech thee, torment me not.
29 (For he had commanded the unclean spirit to come out of the man. For oftentimes it had caught him: and he was kept bound with chains and in fetters; and he brake the bands, and was driven of the devil into the wilderness.)
30 And Jesus asked him, saying, What is thy name? And he said, Legion: because many devils were entered into him.
31 And they besought him that he would not command them to go out into the deep.
32 And there was there an herd of many swine feeding on the mountain: and they besought him that he would suffer them to enter into them. And he suffered them.
33 Then went the devils out of the man, and entered into the swine: and the herd ran violently down a steep place into the lake, and were choked.
34 When they that fed them saw what was done, they fled, and went and told it in the city and in the country.
35 Then they went out to see what was done; and came to Jesus, and found the man, out of whom the devils were departed, sitting at the feet of Jesus, clothed, and in his right mind: and they were afraid.
36 They also which saw it told them by what means he that was possessed of the devils was healed.
37 Then the whole multitude of the country of the

Man and His Word comes to pass. 8.26-39 This section deals with healing of a man called Legion in an area on the eastern side of the sea of Galilee called Gadara(v26). Legion was possessed by demons and was physically, mentally and spiritually ill. He did not live in a house but lived naked in caves where the dead were often buried (v27). Legion could identify the Lord Jesus through the power of the demons (v28). His mental imbalance led others to ostracise him and place him in chains to contain him, but he broke those chains and lived the life of a hermit in the desert (v29). The Lord asked him his name. He gives his true identity- Legion, as he was controlled by many demons (v30). The demons are aware of the superior power of Christ's Word and strangely begs not to be dismissed into the sea (v31) but into the herd of swine (v32), which He permits. The result is that the demons leave Legion at the command of Christ but the swine all die as they stampede into the lake in terror of the demons (v33). This sad story has one big lesson – the salvation of one precious soul is worth more than many animals. The second lesson is that we may have to suffer financial loss if we put spiritual things first. The people come to see an incredible sight - Legion is sitting at the feet of Jesus, not running away, clothed not naked, in his right mind, not mad (v35). This incredible change of state in Legion led the people to be afraid of the power of the Lord Jesus'. If He could change a man like Legion what else would He change? They liked their sinful lifestyle. The Lord left Legion to testify to the great God who had saved him and he began to preach to others about the power of Christ (v39). The simple testimony of how God saved us speaks loudly to people.

8.40-56 Jairus' daughter and the woman with the issue of blood. On return to the other side of the sea a prominent religious man called Jairus fell at the feet of Christ pleading with Him to come to his house as his only daughter was dying (v40-42). On His way to see the little girl He was delayed as a lady who had been haemorrhaging ('issue of blood') for twelve years. She had used up all her savings on doctors ('physicians') without any improvement but believed that she could find healing by simply touching the clothing of Christ' (v43-48). As soon as she did this, her body was healed and the bleeding stopped ('stanched') (v43-44). The Lord Jesus asked who touched Him to draw the lady out to make a public confession of faith in Christ (45-46). The lady realised He knew everything about her and fell at His feet and told Him the whole story (v47). He said to her that she should be full of comfort as not only was her medical problem resolved but she was saved by her faith in Christ. She could now go on and enjoy inner peace with God (v48). Now this delay with the lady meant the Saviour had not yet seen the little girl of Jairus. Jairus receives the news that his daughter is dead (v49).

Gadarenes round about besought him to depart
from them; for they were taken with great fear: and
he went up into the ship, and returned back again.
38 Now the man out of whom the devils were
departed besought him that he might be with him:
but Jesus sent him away, saying,
39 Return to thine own house, and shew how great
things God hath done unto thee. And he went his
way, and published throughout the whole city how
great things Jesus had done unto him.

The Incurable Woman Healed and Jairus' Daughter Raised

40 And it came to pass, that, when Jesus was
returned, the people gladly received him: for they
were all waiting for him.
41 And, behold, there came a man named Jairus, and
he was a ruler of the synagogue: and he fell down at
Jesus' feet, and besought him that he would come
into his house:
42 For he had one only daughter, about twelve
years of age, and she lay a dying. But as he went
the people thronged him.
43 And a woman having an issue of blood twelve
years, which had spent all her living upon physicians,
neither could be healed of any,
44 Came behind him, and touched the border of
his garment: and immediately her issue of blood
stanched.
45 And Jesus said, Who touched me? When all
denied, Peter and they that were with him said,
Master, the multitude throng thee and press thee,
and sayest thou, Who touched me?
46 And Jesus said, Somebody hath touched me: for
I perceive that virtue is gone out of me.
47 And when the woman saw that she was not hid,
she came trembling, and falling down before him,
she declared unto him before all the people for
what cause she had touched him, and how she was
healed immediately.
48 And he said unto her, Daughter, be of good
comfort: thy faith hath made thee whole; go in
peace.

49 While he yet spake, there cometh one from the
ruler of the synagogue's house, saying to him, Thy
daughter is dead; trouble not the Master.
50 But when Jesus heard it, he answered him, saying,
Fear not: believe only, and she shall be made whole.
51 And when he came into the house, he suffered no
man to go in, save Peter, and James, and John, and
the father and the mother of the maiden.
52 And all wept, and bewailed her: but he said, Weep
not; she is not dead, but sleepeth.
53 And they laughed him to scorn, knowing that
she was dead.
54 And he put them all out, and took her by the
hand, and called, saying, Maid, arise.
55 And her spirit came again, and she arose
straightway: and he commanded to give her meat.
56 And her parents were astonished: but he charged
them that they should tell no man what was done.

The Lord Jesus told him not to be afraid but believe His Word and his girl would be made whole. When He arrived at Jairus' house He only permitted three disciples to be with Him and the father and mother. He said to the mourners outside that the girl was not dead but only sleeping (v52). The response to His Word was mockery (v53). He puts all unbelievers and scoffers out and takes the little girl by the hand saying 'Little girl, get up' (v54). The little girl got up immediately and the Lord commanded that she got a good meal (v55). Jairus and his wife were amazed at Christ but He instructed them not to go about speaking to everyone about it. This was true compassion and humility. He was not here for His own glory but for the glory of God.

Reflective Questions and Notes

A. What is the main point of the parable of the sower? v4-15

B. Who are the Lord's family? v21

C. What calmed the storm on the lake and healed Legion's mind? v22-40

D. What was the sin of the mourners at Jairus' house? v52-53

Luke 9

The Sending Out of the Twelve

1 Then he called his twelve disciples together, and gave them power and authority over all devils, and to cure diseases.

2 And he sent them to preach the kingdom of God, and to heal the sick.

3 And he said unto them, Take nothing for your journey, neither staves, nor scrip, neither bread, neither money; neither have two coats apiece.

4 And whatsoever house ye enter into, there abide, and thence depart.

5 And whosoever will not receive you, when ye go out of that city, shake off the very dust from your feet for a testimony against them.

6 And they departed, and went through the towns, preaching the gospel, and healing every where.

7 Now Herod the tetrarch heard of all that was done by him: and he was perplexed, because that it was said of some, that John was risen from the dead;

8 And of some, that Elias had appeared; and of others, that one of the old prophets was risen again.

9 And Herod said, John have I beheaded: but who is this, of whom I hear such things? And he desired to see him.

Feeding of the Five Thousand

10 And the apostles, when they were returned, told him all that they had done. And he took them, and went aside privately into a desert place belonging to the city called Bethsaida.

11 And the people, when they knew it, followed him: and he received them, and spake unto them of the kingdom of God, and healed them that had need of healing.

12 And when the day began to wear away, then came the twelve, and said unto him, Send the multitude away, that they may go into the towns and country round about, and lodge, and get victuals: for we are here in a desert place.

13 But he said unto them, Give ye them to eat. And they said, We have no more but five loaves and two

Chapters 9-10 Discipleship

9.1-11 The sending out of the twelve. The twelve disciples were able to do miracles but only so that it confirmed the truth of their main mission – to preach the kingdom of God (v1-2). The preaching of the Word of God carries the power to transform lives. They were to move out in faith believing that support ('staves'- i.e. a staff), food, finance and additional clothing would be provided (v3). They were to accept shelter (v4) and where they were rejected then God would deal directly with those individuals (v5). Their message was not to be parochial – it was for everyone, everywhere (V6). Herod heard through the preaching of the disciples more about Christ (People in high positions and even enemies of the gospel need the Word of God as well) and he started to get unnerved wondering if John the Baptist had been resurrected (v7). It was not the first time (nor will be the last) that people who are unsaved take a morbid interest in the afterlife and occult. Some said that the Lord Jesus was Elijah (Elias – I Kings 17) or a prophet (v8). Herod knew that he had personally beheaded John the Baptist and his conscience was bothering him. He longed to see the Lord Jesus but more out of curiosity than spiritual conviction (v9). The disciples return from their preaching tour and related all the events to the Lord. He spends some time with them in private. All disciples need this (v10). The crowds gather to Christ and He taught them about the kingdom of God and healed those in need.

9.12-17 The feeding of the 5000.

As the evening drew closer the disciples' counsel to the Saviour was to send the crowd away from the desert (v10, 12) so that they could get accommodation for the night and some food ('victuals'). His reply is amazing – 'You give them to eat'! He did not want the people to leave. They reply that they only have 5 small loaves and 2 fish (v13). The Lord asks that they arrange the company of possibly 10000 plus (if you include women and children) into fifties, sitting down (v14-15). He blesses what they had and distributes the food to the crowd, through the disciples (v16). Everyone ate, were full and the food left over filled twelve baskets (v17). When disciples give what they have to the Lord, He multiplies it and uses it to be a blessing to others.

9.18-26 The Lord's teaching to His own disciples about Who He is. During prayer, He asks who the people think He is (v18), they reply in a similar way to 9.7-8 (v19) He then becomes personal asking who they thought He was. Peter's answer is sublime – the Christ of God (v20). He reminds them that the time was not now for this truth to be fully revealed to the world (v21) as first of all He must suffer, be rejected and die but on the third day rise again (v22). His disciples must be ready for a similar path – a path of self-denial and suffering (v23). He added the counterintuitive promise that those who lose for Christ's sake will gain eternally (v24). Indeed, He added, if we were to have all the world's gold, fame and power and lose our soul we would be eternally the loser (v25). Spiritual things are infinitely more important than the material. To be ashamed of Christ and His Word will lead to

fishes; except we should go and buy meat for all this people.

14 For they were about five thousand men. And he said to his disciples, Make them sit down by fifties in a company.

15 And they did so, and made them all sit down.

16 Then he took the five loaves and the two fishes, and looking up to heaven, he blessed them, and brake, and gave to the disciples to set before the multitude.

17 And they did eat, and were all filled: and there was taken up of fragments that remained to them twelve baskets.

Peter's Testimony to Christ

18 And it came to pass, as he was alone praying, his disciples were with him: and he asked them, saying, Whom say the people that I am?

19 They answering said, John the Baptist; but some say, Elias; and others say, that one of the old prophets is risen again.

20 He said unto them, But whom say ye that I am? Peter answering said, The Christ of God.

21 And he straitly charged them, and commanded them to tell no man that thing;

The First Prediction of Death and Resurrection

22 Saying, The Son of man must suffer many things, and be rejected of the elders and chief priests and scribes, and be slain, and be raised the third day.

The Call to True Discipleship

23 And he said to them all, If any man will come after me, let him deny himself, and take up his cross daily, and follow me.

24 For whosoever will save his life shall lose it: but whosoever will lose his life for my sake, the same shall save it.

25 For what is a man advantaged, if he gain the whole world, and lose himself, or be cast away?

26 For whosoever shall be ashamed of me and of my words, of him shall the Son of man be ashamed, when he shall come in his own glory, and in his Father's, and of the holy angels.

The Mount of Transfiguration

27 But I tell you of a truth, there be some standing

here, which shall not taste of death, till they see the kingdom of God.

28 And it came to pass about an eight days after these sayings, he took Peter and John and James, and went up into a mountain to pray.

29 And as he prayed, the fashion of his countenance was altered, and his raiment was white and glistering.

30 And, behold, there talked with him two men, which were Moses and Elias:

31 Who appeared in glory, and spake of his decease which he should accomplish at Jerusalem.

32 But Peter and they that were with him were heavy with sleep: and when they were awake, they saw his glory, and the two men that stood with him.

33 And it came to pass, as they departed from him, Peter said unto Jesus, Master, it is good for us to be here: and let us make three tabernacles; one for thee, and one for Moses, and one for Elias: not knowing what he said.

34 While he thus spake, there came a cloud, and overshadowed them: and they feared as they entered into the cloud.

35 And there came a voice out of the cloud, saying, This is my beloved Son: hear him.

36 And when the voice was past, Jesus was found alone. And they kept it close, and told no man in those days any of those things which they had seen.

The Demon-Possessed Child Healed

37 And it came to pass, that on the next day, when they were come down from the hill, much people met him.

38 And, behold, a man of the company cried out, saying, Master, I beseech thee, look upon my son: for he is mine only child.

39 And, lo, a spirit taketh him, and he suddenly crieth out; and it teareth him that he foameth again, and bruising him hardly departeth from him.

40 And I besought thy disciples to cast him out; and they could not.

41 And Jesus answering said, O faithless and perverse generation, how long shall I be with you, and suffer you? Bring thy son hither.

the Lord Jesus, the Father and angels being ashamed of us on the day of His return. How solemn (v26)

9.27- 36 The Lord on Mount Transfiguration. The Lord having taught of His return to set up His kingdom says that there are disciples with Him who would see the kingdom before they died (v27). He then gives three of them an opportunity to see a preview of the Kingdom of God eight days later (v28). Up a mountain, when in prayer, Peter, James and John see His face changing ('countenance') and His clothing ('raiment') as white and glistering (v29). Moses and Elijah appear with Him in glory to talk to the Saviour (v30) about His death ('exodus') at Jerusalem (v30-31). Peter and the others see the glory of Christ and His kingdom and in his nervousness and uncertainty to know what to say, Peter responds by saying they will build three altars for worship. He gave the Lord the first place but He did not give Him the only place (v33). God responds by coming down in a cloud and speaking of His Son in the noblest of terms. There is no other with Him to be compared. He must have the first place and only place (v34-35). The cloud disappears, and the disciples are left with Christ alone. They had been given a vison of His future glory in His kingdom and they would never forget it.

9.37-50 The healing of the demon possessed boy at the bottom of the mountain. There was glory at the top of the mountain and gloom at the bottom. A man's only child was demon possessed, fitting and foaming at the mouth, crying out in fear and being hurt (v37-39). The nine disciples at the bottom of the mountain had tried to help but failed (v40). The Lord rebukes the lack of faith of His own and asks to see the boy (v41 – 'hither' means 'here'). As the boy arrived the demon threw the boy on the ground convulsing. With one word the boy was healed and restored to his father in his right mind (v42). This resulted in much amazement at the power of God (v43). The Lord used this time as an opportunity to speak about His rejection (v44), not His future reign. This boy was a perfect example of what was wrong with the world and why He had come to deliver people from their sin. This meant He had to die and endure rejection. This message was not understood (v45).

9.46-61 The Lord's teaching on Christian character. Incredibly the fact that three disciples were up the mountain with the Lord and those below could not heal the boy seems to have led to a discussion of who was the most important to the Lord (v46). The Lord immediately deals with this pride by taking a child to illustrate humility (v47). True greatness is seen in true, child-like humility, working for the Name of Christ, and taking the least place. The way up is the way down (v48). John wonders about those who do miracles in the Name of Christ but they do not follow the Lord like the twelve do. John spoke against them (v49). The Lord teaches him that he shouldn't do this as 'those that are not against us are for us'. John needed wisdom (v50). At this time the Lord set His face to go to Jerusalem to die (v51). We are now entering the last few months of the Lord's life on earth. Disciples were sent ahead into Samaria to prepare as He moved south towards Jerusalem (v52).

42 And as he was yet a coming, the devil threw him
down, and tare him. And Jesus rebuked the unclean
spirit, and healed the child, and delivered him again
to his father.

The Second Prediction of the Lord's Death

43 And they were all amazed at the mighty power
of God. But while they wondered every one at all
things which Jesus did, he said unto his disciples,
44 Let these sayings sink down into your ears: for the
Son of man shall be delivered into the hands of men.
45 But they understood not this saying, and it was
hid from them, that they perceived it not: and they
feared to ask him of that saying.

The Reasoning about Who Would Be the Greatest

46 Then there arose a reasoning among them, which
of them should be greatest.
47 And Jesus, perceiving the thought of their heart,
took a child, and set him by him,
48 And said unto them, Whosoever shall receive
this child in my name receiveth me: and whosoever
shall receive me receiveth him that sent me: for he
that is least among you all, the same shall be great.
49 And John answered and said, Master, we saw one
casting out devils in thy name; and we forbad him,
because he followeth not with us.
50 And Jesus said unto him, Forbid him not: for he
that is not against us is for us.

The Departure from Galilee

51 And it came to pass, when the time was come
that he should be received up, he stedfastly set his
face to go to Jerusalem,

The Rejection of the Lord in Samaria

52 And sent messengers before his face: and they
went, and entered into a village of the Samaritans,
to make ready for him.
53 And they did not receive him, because his face
was as though he would go to Jerusalem.
54 And when his disciples James and John saw this, they
said, Lord, wilt thou that we command fire to come down
from heaven, and consume them, even as Elias did?
55 But he turned, and rebuked them, and said, Ye
know not what manner of spirit ye are of.

56 For the Son of man is not come to destroy men's
lives, but to save them. And they went to another
village.

True Discipleship

57 And it came to pass, that, as they went in the way,
a certain man said unto him, Lord, I will follow thee
whithersoever thou goest.
58 And Jesus said unto him, Foxes have holes, and
birds of the air have nests; but the Son of man hath
not where to lay his head.
59 And he said unto another, Follow me. But he
said, Lord, suffer me first to go and bury my father.
60 Jesus said unto him, Let the dead bury their dead:
but go thou and preach the kingdom of God.
61 And another also said, Lord, I will follow thee;
but let me first go bid them farewell, which are at
home at my house.
62 And Jesus said unto him, No man, having put his
hand to the plough, and looking back, is fit for the
kingdom of God.

The Samaritans refused access as they perceived Him to be friendly towards the Jews, with whom they were in dispute (v53). James and John's response is to, Elijah-like, wish fire to consume them for dishonouring the Lord (v54). The Lord once again rebukes their character this time not for a lack of humility or wisdom but now for a lack of grace (v55). The Lord Jesus had come to save people not destroy them (v56). As He went to the other village a man said he would be prepared to follow the Lord anywhere He went (v57). The Lord answered by telling him He did not have a home unlike birds or animals (v58). The character He was looking from His disciples was love for Him and not love for this world. The Lord asked another to follow Him but he replied that his family were too important to him, once they had all died he would follow the Lord (v59) and another wanted to go back to the family first before following. The Lord replied that following Him required sacrifice and He must have the first place (v59-62).

Reflective Questions and Notes

A. After their preaching tour where do the disciples return and what do they do? v1-11

B. When they were alone with Him what did the Lord ensure the disciples understood about Himself? v18-26?

C. What did the Lord mean in His statement of v27, and how was this carried out? v27-36

D. What lesson did the Lord teach them from the child of v42 and the child of v47?

E. Why is verse 51 an important time note?

Luke 10

The Sending of the Seventy

1 After these things the Lord appointed other seventy also, and sent them two and two before his face into every city and place, whither he himself would come.

2 Therefore said he unto them, The harvest truly is great, but the labourers are few: pray ye therefore the Lord of the harvest, that he would send forth labourers into his harvest.

3 Go your ways: behold, I send you forth as lambs among wolves.

4 Carry neither purse, nor scrip, nor shoes: and salute no man by the way.

5 And into whatsoever house ye enter, first say, Peace be to this house.

6 And if the son of peace be there, your peace shall rest upon it: if not, it shall turn to you again.

7 And in the same house remain, eating and drinking such things as they give: for the labourer is worthy of his hire. Go not from house to house.

8 And into whatsoever city ye enter, and they receive you, eat such things as are set before you:

9 And heal the sick that are therein, and say unto them, The kingdom of God is come nigh unto you.

10 But into whatsoever city ye enter, and they receive you not, go your ways out into the streets of the same, and say,

11 Even the very dust of your city, which cleaveth on us, we do wipe off against you: notwithstanding be ye sure of this, that the kingdom of God is come nigh unto you.

12 But I say unto you, that it shall be more tolerable in that day for Sodom, than for that city.

The Pronouncement of judgment on Privileged Cities

13 Woe unto thee, Chorazin! woe unto thee, Bethsaida! for if the mighty works had been done in Tyre and Sidon, which have been done in you, they had a great while ago repented, sitting in sackcloth and ashes.

14 But it shall be more tolerable for Tyre and Sidon at the judgment, than for you.

Chapters 9-10 Discipleship

10.1 -16 The sending out of the seventy disciples. The disciples are sent out as He makes His last journey towards Jerusalem (v1; 9. 51). The Lord saw humanity as a great field of souls that needed harvesting with so few labourers to do it. He invites prayer that the Lord of the harvest would send more labourers into the field, reminding us that God hears prayer (v2). He sends the 70 disciples like meek lambs in a ferocious wolf-like world (v3). They were to go in faith taking no extra money, additional bag ('scrip') or another pair of shoes. They were not to idle but to be ambassadors for the king (v4). Any house that they entered they were to bless with peace and if the house showed peace to them then the household would be blessed, otherwise the blessing would leave the house when they left (v5-6). They were to accept provisions as from the Lord and eat whatever they were given but not go from house to house begging from people (v7-8). They were to be known by their actions and words - heal people who are in need and remind them that the Kingdom of God had come; the King was alive (v8-9). If they were not received then judgment would pass on that place (even more than Sodom in Gen. 19) but their message about the kingdom would still not change (v10-12). The Lord proceeds to utter woes of judgment on those places that reject His disciples (v13-16). He singles out the cities He had preached in along the side of Lake Galilee for special judgment (v13) for not repenting. Even ancient cities like Tyre and Sidon, notorious for their sin and judgment, would have repented if they had seen the miracles Bethsaida, Capernaum and Chorazin had witnessed (v13,15)! He warns of future judgment and explains there will be differences in judgment according to responsibility (v14). He warns that this holds true for the disciples. To hear them speak is to hear Him and to despise them is to despise Him. How solemn.

10.17-24 The Seventy return. The Seventy seem to be impressed with their ability to do miracles in the Name of Christ (v17). The Lord reminds them of Satan's fall – a former archangel (Ezekiel 28) who fell through pride (v18). He tells them that although they have been given great powers (v19,) the matter that they should really rejoice in is this that their names are written in heaven (v20) – the grace of God. The name of every person who comes to Christ for salvation is written in heaven (Rev 20. 15) The Lord thanks His Father in prayer that these great truths have been revealed to the simple fishermen of Galilee who are like babes compared to the kings and rich people of the earth. God has chosen humility to be the instrument to bless the world (v21). The Son of God's purpose in coming to earth was to reveal the Father (v22) and so He blesses the disciples for seeing something of His glory (v23) which He says has been denied the leaders of this world (v24).

10.25-37. The parable of the Good Samaritan was told to a religious man (lawyer i.e. student of Old Testament) who thought he could keep the law of God (v25-29). The man thought his neighbour was someone that he could help. He learns

15 And thou, Capernaum, which art exalted to heaven, shalt be thrust down to hell.

16 He that heareth you heareth me; and he that despiseth you despiseth me; and he that despiseth me despiseth him that sent me.

The True Causes of joy

17 And the seventy returned again with joy, saying, Lord, even the devils are subject unto us through thy name.

18 And he said unto them, I beheld Satan as lightning fall from heaven.

19 Behold, I give unto you power to tread on serpents and scorpions, and over all the power of the enemy: and nothing shall by any means hurt you.

20 Notwithstanding in this rejoice not, that the spirits are subject unto you; but rather rejoice, because your names are written in heaven.

21 In that hour Jesus rejoiced in spirit, and said, I thank thee, O Father, Lord of heaven and earth, that thou hast hid these things from the wise and prudent, and hast revealed them unto babes: even so, Father; for so it seemed good in thy sight.

22 All things are delivered to me of my Father: and no man knoweth who the Son is, but the Father; and who the Father is, but the Son, and he to whom the Son will reveal him.

23 And he turned him unto his disciples, and said privately, Blessed are the eyes which see the things that ye see:

24 For I tell you, that many prophets and kings have desired to see those things which ye see, and have not seen them; and to hear those things which ye hear, and have not heard them.

A Lawyer's Question

25 And, behold, a certain lawyer stood up, and tempted him, saying, Master, what shall I do to inherit eternal life?

26 He said unto him, What is written in the law? how readest thou?

27 And he answering said, Thou shalt love the Lord thy God with all thy heart, and with all thy soul, and

Reflective Questions and Notes

A. What were the features that were to mark the disciples of Christ? v1-16

B. What is even more important than being able to perform miracles? v18-21

C. Why was the parable of the Good Samaritan told? Why did the outcome shock the lawyer? v25-37

D. What was the one thing that Mary had that was vital over all other things in life? v38-41

Chapter 11 Prayer and our relationship with God.
11.1-4 The pattern prayer of Christ. The disciples said, 'Teach us to pray' and not 'Teach us how to pray'. When they heard Him pray it was if they had never prayed before. He taught them that prayer consisted of a (i) relationship 'Father' (ii) reverence and awe e.g. 'hallowed - honoured' (v2);
(iii) requests of a material, moral and spiritual nature (v3, v4)
(iii) repentance and petition to preserve from future sin (v4) and (iv) renewal, a future hope ('thy kingdom come'.
11.5-13. The Lord teaching on how to make requests in prayer is through a relationship with God. The Lord told the parable of the man whose friend comes at the middle of the night to boldly make a request from a friend. Despite the harassing and persistent approach and unsuitable circumstances his friend helps him out and gives him everything he needs (v5-8). If this is true of earthly relationships how much more is it true of our relationship with God the Father. The Lord is showing the disciples the true nature of their relationship with the Father – friends. We need to ask, seek, knock and we shall receive (v9-10).

V11-13 The Lord explained that when we make requests in prayer the relationship is of children, speaking to their Father. If a caring earthly father would not give his children anything that could harm then how much more will God t

Luke 11

Teaching on Prayer

1 And it came to pass, that, as he was praying in a
certain place, when he ceased, one of his disciples
said unto him, Lord, teach us to pray, as John also
taught his disciples.
2 And he said unto them, When ye pray, say, Our
Father which art in heaven, Hallowed be thy name.
Thy kingdom come. Thy will be done, as in heaven,
so in earth.
3 Give us day by day our daily bread.
4 And forgive us our sins; for we also forgive every
one that is indebted to us. And lead us not into
temptation; but deliver us from evil.

The Parable of the Needy Friend

5 And he said unto them, Which of you shall have a
friend, and shall go unto him at midnight, and say
unto him, Friend, lend me three loaves;
6 For a friend of mine in his journey is come to me,
and I have nothing to set before him?
7 And he from within shall answer and say, Trouble
me not: the door is now shut, and my children are
with me in bed; I cannot rise and give thee.
8 I say unto you, Though he will not rise and give
him, because he is his friend, yet because of his
importunity he will rise and give him as many as
he needeth.
9 And I say unto you, Ask, and it shall be given
you; seek, and ye shall find; knock, and it shall be
opened unto you.
10 For every one that asketh receiveth; and he that
seeketh findeth; and to him that knocketh it shall
be opened.
11 If a son shall ask bread of any of you that is a
father, will he give him a stone? or if he ask a fish,
will he for a fish give him a serpent?
12 Or if he shall ask an egg, will he offer him a
scorpion?
13 If ye then, being evil, know how to give good
gifts unto your children: how much more shall your
heavenly Father give the Holy Spirit to them that
ask him?

The Kingdom of Darkness

14 And he was casting out a devil, and it was dumb. And it came to pass, when the devil was gone out, the dumb spake; and the people wondered.

15 But some of them said, He casteth out devils through Beelzebub the chief of the devils.

16 And others, tempting him, sought of him a sign from heaven.

17 But he, knowing their thoughts, said unto them, Every kingdom divided against itself is brought to desolation; and a house divided against a house falleth.

18 If Satan also be divided against himself, how shall his kingdom stand? because ye say that I cast out devils through Beelzebub.

19 And if I by Beelzebub cast out devils, by whom do your sons cast them out? therefore shall they be your judges.

20 But if I with the finger of God cast out devils, no doubt the kingdom of God is come upon you.

21 When a strong man armed keepeth his palace, his goods are in peace:

22 But when a stronger than he shall come upon him, and overcome him, he taketh from him all his armour wherein he trusted, and divideth his spoils.

23 He that is not with me is against me: and he that gathereth not with me scattereth.

24 When the unclean spirit is gone out of a man, he walketh through dry places, seeking rest; and finding none, he saith, I will return unto my house whence I came out.

25 And when he cometh, he findeth it swept and garnished.

26 Then goeth he, and taketh to him seven other spirits more wicked than himself; and they enter in, and dwell there: and the last state of that man is worse than the first.

27 And it came to pass, as he spake these things, a certain woman of the company lifted up her voice, and said unto him, Blessed is the womb that bare thee, and the paps which thou hast sucked.

28 But he said, Yea rather, blessed are they that hear the word of God, and keep it.

he Father never give us anything that could harm us – in fact He will give us the Holy Spirit.

11.14-26 The Lord then taught lessons on how our requests can be answered – through the power of Christ alone as King in His kingdom. After healing a man of a demon and granting him his speech there were those religious people who said the Lord's ability to dispense such blessing came from the Devil. Beelzebub was used as a name for the Devil (v15). The Lord dismisses this possibility by (i) logic - saying that if the Devil casts out the Devil then his kingdom is divided (v17-18); (ii) by inference – inviting them to consider by what power their own people cast out demons through (v19). He then makes an incredible claim for His own person, stating that if it is the evident finger of God at work through His miracles then the kingdom of God is amongst them (v20). He, as King, has evidently greater power than the Devil (the strong man) and is able to overcome him and remove from him those he has captured ('his spoils' - v21-22). If they (the religious Pharisees) will not accept Him then they are against Him and will be scattered and judged (v23). He then explains how demons sometimes leave a person allowing them to get 'cleaned up' a little (v25). The person can believe that they have the power in themselves to live for God but have, however, never known the power of Christ in their lives. The demons return, and the end state of that person is worse than ever.

11.27-36 The Lord explains that we receive blessing from God – through obedience and faith in His Word and a spiritual relationship with Christ. A lady blessed the womb and breasts ('paps') of His mother Mary. He reminded the lady that although Mary was blessed so are all who hear the Word of God and obey it (v28). He warned that the current generation would have no special sign but the sign of Jonah the prophet (v28- an Old Testament book called Jonah explains this example). The men of Nineveh heard Jonah preach and repented (v32 – see Jonah Chapter 4). What about this generation who heard the Son of God preach? Likewise, the Queen of Sheba would condemn them as she came a long journey to hear King Solomon (1 Kings 10. 1-10) and now the greatest King was in their midst? What would be their response? True repentance and true affection for Christ is not hidden, it is like a well-positioned light – all can see it (v33). He warned lest any of them should miss the light of the world and be in the darkness of their sin (v34-36).

Great Examples from the Old Testament

29 And when the people were gathered thick
together, he began to say, This is an evil generation:
they seek a sign; and there shall no sign be given it,
but the sign of Jonas the prophet.
30 For as Jonas was a sign unto the Ninevites, so
shall also the Son of man be to this generation.
31 The queen of the south shall rise up in the
judgment with the men of this generation, and
condemn them: for she came from the utmost parts
of the earth to hear the wisdom of Solomon; and,
behold, a greater than Solomon is here.
32 The men of Nineve shall rise up in the judgment
with this generation, and shall condemn it: for they
repented at the preaching of Jonas; and, behold, a
greater than Jonas is here.

The Single Eye

33 No man, when he hath lighted a candle, putteth
it in a secret place, neither under a bushel, but on
a candlestick, that they which come in may see the
light.
34 The light of the body is the eye: therefore when
thine eye is single, thy whole body also is full of
light; but when thine eye is evil, thy body also is
full of darkness.
35 Take heed therefore that the light which is in
thee be not darkness.
36 If thy whole body therefore be full of light, having
no part dark, the whole shall be full of light, as when
the bright shining of a candle doth give thee light.

11.37-54. The Lord taught the danger of making out we have a relationship with God when we do not. The incident that draws out this teaching is when a Pharisee asks Him to dinner. The Lord deliberately does not wash His hands before the meal causing the religious man such astonishment. The Lord uses this to teach him and all religious people a big lesson. If they are so anxious to be clean outwardly washing hands and cleaning plates ('platter') and

The Pharisees and Lawyers Denounced

37 And as he spake, a certain Pharisee besought
him to dine with him: and he went in, and sat down
to meat.
38 And when the Pharisee saw it, he marvelled that
he had not first washed before dinner.
39 And the Lord said unto him, Now do ye Pharisees
make clean the outside of the cup and the platter;
but your inward part is full of ravening and
wickedness.
40 Ye fools, did not he that made that which is
without make that which is within also?

41 But rather give alms of such things as ye have;
and, behold, all things are clean unto you.
42 But woe unto you, Pharisees! for ye tithe mint and
rue and all manner of herbs, and pass over judgment
and the love of God: these ought ye to have done,
and not to leave the other undone.
43 Woe unto you, Pharisees! for ye love the
uppermost seats in the synagogues, and greetings
in the markets.
44 Woe unto you, scribes and Pharisees, hypocrites!
for ye are as graves which appear not, and the men
that walk over them are not aware of them.
45 Then answered one of the lawyers, and said unto
him, Master, thus saying thou reproachest us also.
46 And he said, Woe unto you also, ye lawyers! for
ye lade men with burdens grievous to be borne,
and ye yourselves touch not the burdens with one
of your fingers.
47 Woe unto you! for ye build the sepulchres of the
prophets, and your fathers killed them.
48 Truly ye bear witness that ye allow the deeds of
your fathers: for they indeed killed them, and ye
build their sepulchres.
49 Therefore also said the wisdom of God, I will send
them prophets and apostles, and some of them they
shall slay and persecute:
50 That the blood of all the prophets, which was
shed from the foundation of the world, may be
required of this generation;
51 From the blood of Abel unto the blood of
Zacharias which perished between the altar and the
temple: verily I say unto you, It shall be required of
this generation.
52 Woe unto you, lawyers! for ye have taken away
the key of knowledge: ye entered not in yourselves,
and them that were entering in ye hindered.
53 And as he said these things unto them, the scribes
and the Pharisees began to urge him vehemently,
and to provoke him to speak of many things:
54 Laying wait for him, and seeking to catch
something out of his mouth, that they might accuse
him.

cups etc why do they not show the same concern about their inward thoughts and motives. Giving away money is good but what about giving of your heart? Tithing of herbs like mint and rue are all to be admired but what did they know of the righteousness and love of God? He is moved to warn them of coming judgment for such serious sin of neglecting such major truth in a series of six woes (v42, 43, 44, 46, 47, 52). The first three are targeted at the Pharisees – a particularly strict and legalistic sect of Judaism. They liked public place and honour (v44); outward purity – despite inward deadness (v44). He turns to the lawyers – those who considered themselves to be experts in Holy Scripture. He warns against the unnecessary legal burdens they place on people (v46) and the hypocritical veneration of the prophets who were killed for the testimony to the truth by their fathers (v47-51). This had been their history from the beginning of their Bibles at the dawn of time (Genesis 4 - 'Abel' killed by his brother Cain) to the last book in the Jewish Old Testament Scriptures (2 Chronicles – where the stoning of the prophet Zechariah is mentioned). He finally warns that the lawyers have taken away the key to knowledge by refusing to accept His testimony (v52). This very direct challenge to the religious leaders does not lead to repentance but attacks on the person of Christ by stealth. None of their trick questions or approaches have any effect. They could not find anything in His life that they could condemn.

Reflective Questions and Notes

A. What are the essential features of prayer? v1-4

B. How does the parable of the three friends relate to prayer? v5-13

C. Who has the power to answer prayer? How does the Lord illustrate this? v14-36

D. What did the Lord deliberately not do when He went to Simon the Pharisee's house? Why? v37-54

Luke 12

The Warning Against the Leaven of the Pharisees

1 In the mean time, when there were gathered together an innumerable multitude of people, insomuch that they trode one upon another, he began to say unto his disciples first of all, Beware ye of the leaven of the Pharisees, which is hypocrisy.
2 For there is nothing covered, that shall not be revealed; neither hid, that shall not be known.
3 Therefore whatsoever ye have spoken in darkness shall be heard in the light; and that which ye have spoken in the ear in closets shall be proclaimed upon the housetops.
4 And I say unto you my friends, Be not afraid of them that kill the body, and after that have no more that they can do.
5 But I will forewarn you whom ye shall fear: Fear him, which after he hath killed hath power to cast into hell; yea, I say unto you, Fear him.
6 Are not five sparrows sold for two farthings, and not one of them is forgotten before God?
7 But even the very hairs of your head are all numbered. Fear not therefore: ye are of more value than many sparrows.
8 Also I say unto you, Whosoever shall confess me before men, him shall the Son of man also confess before the angels of God:
9 But he that denieth me before men shall be denied before the angels of God.
10 And whosoever shall speak a word against the Son of man, it shall be forgiven him: but unto him that blasphemeth against the Holy Ghost it shall not be forgiven.
11 And when they bring you unto the synagogues, and unto magistrates, and powers, take ye no thought how or what thing ye shall answer, or what ye shall say:
12 For the Holy Ghost shall teach you in the same hour what ye ought to say.
13 And one of the company said unto him, Master, speak to my brother, that he divide the inheritance with me.

Chapter 12: Perspectives and Mindsets

12.1 -12 Hypocrisy

12.1 'In the meantime' – during the very time that the Pharisees were watching Him to see if He made a mistake; 'trode' means 'tread';'leaven' – yeast; often used as a picture of evil. In the case of the Pharisees, hypocrisy.

12.2-3 Christ urges His hearers to be clear and transparent warning of a day when our hearts, motives and actions will all be revealed.

12.4-5 Christ also urges His hearers to be courageous, fearing God rather than men with their religious persecution. The worst that the Pharisees could do would be to kill them but God deals with the body and the soul.

12.6 -10 Christ urges His hearers to confess Him reminding them of how valuable they are to Him. He knows all about their circumstances and will in turn confess them before the angels. The corollary is that those deny Him will in turn be denied in heaven and those who ascribe to the Lord Jesus a spirit of evil rather than the Holy Spirit will not be forgiven.

12.11-12 Christ encourages those who will be persecuted for His sake that they will be given special help to testify when summoned to the tribunals and courts. They will be taught by the Holy Spirit the exact words to say.

12.13- 34 Covetousness

12.13-14 The incident of being asked to get involved in family squabbles over the division of inheritance was used by the Lord to speak about covetousness.

12.15 The Lord taught that we cannot measure our life by material things.
12.16-21 Parable of the rich fool. This parable illustrates the folly of thinking only in a material manner. There was nothing wrong with the idea of building bigger barns, it was the material and sensual attitude of the man that was the problem (v19). This man did not live for God and had no thought of giving thanks to God for His goodness to him or seeking His guidance on his next steps. In the end the man who lived for self and was given so much in his life lost the only thing he had that was of any real value – his soul (v20). True riches are eternal (v21).

12.22-34. The Lord turns to the disciples to emphasise the truth of depending on God for everything and not being preoccupied by material things.
12.23 'meat' means food; 'raiment' means clothes.
12.24-31 The Lord Illustrates His teaching through the ravens and lilies. Ravens do not plough or sow or reap, nor have any barn and yet are still fed by God. Lilies do not make their own clothes and yet their beauty and glory is magnificent. It is a reminder to them of God's goodness in providing food and clothing for them (v24-28). It is not, however, encouraging anyone to be lazy. Instead what is being emphasised is that the principle of blessing is based on God's grace and not of human effort or works (Eph 2. 8). The

14 And he said unto him, Man, who made me a judge or a divider over you?

The Parable of the Rich Businessman

15 **And he said unto them, Take heed, and beware of covetousness: for a man's life consisteth not in the abundance of the things which he possesseth.**
16 And he spake a parable unto them, saying, The ground of a certain rich man brought forth plentifully:
17 And he thought within himself, saying, What shall I do, because I have no room where to bestow my fruits?
18 And he said, This will I do: I will pull down my barns, and build greater; and there will I bestow all my fruits and my goods.
19 And I will say to my soul, Soul, thou hast much goods laid up for many years; take thine ease, eat, drink, and be merry.
20 But God said unto him, Thou fool, this night thy soul shall be required of thee: then whose shall those things be, which thou hast provided?
21 So is he that layeth up treasure for himself, and is not rich toward God.
22 And he said unto his disciples, Therefore I say unto you, Take no thought for your life, what ye shall eat; neither for the body, what ye shall put on.
23 The life is more than meat, and the body is more than raiment.
24 Consider the ravens: for they neither sow nor reap; which neither have storehouse nor barn; and God feedeth them: how much more are ye better than the fowls?
25 And which of you with taking thought can add to his stature one cubit?
26 If ye then be not able to do that thing which is least, why take ye thought for the rest?
27 Consider the lilies how they grow: they toil not, they spin not; and yet I say unto you, that Solomon in all his glory was not arrayed like one of these.
28 If then God so clothe the grass, which is to day in the field, and to morrow is cast into the oven; how much more will he clothe you, O ye of little faith?

29 And seek not ye what ye shall eat, or what ye shall drink, neither be ye of doubtful mind.
30 For all these things do the nations of the world seek after: and your Father knoweth that ye have need of these things.
31 But rather seek ye the kingdom of God; and all these things shall be added unto you.
32 Fear not, little flock; for it is your Father's good pleasure to give you the kingdom.
33 Sell that ye have, and give alms; provide yourselves bags which wax not old, a treasure in the heavens that faileth not, where no thief approacheth, neither moth corrupteth.
34 For where your treasure is, there will your heart be also.

Lord is also warning that we can be consumed with the physical (food, drink, clothes) and ignore the eternal (v28-29).

12.30 Disciples are asked to be different to the world in their motivation ('seek after').

12.31-34 Disciples are asked to be motivated and inspired by the kingdom of God. This is to be their priority. It is the Father's pleasure to give them a spiritual inheritance. He encourages them to have a loose hold on material things on earth and go in for the heavenly treasure. Their heart is where their treasure is.

Men that Wait for their Lord

35 Let your loins be girded about, and your lights burning;
36 And ye yourselves like unto men that wait for their lord, when he will return from the wedding; that when he cometh and knocketh, they may open unto him immediately.
37 Blessed are those servants, whom the lord when he cometh shall find watching: verily I say unto you, that he shall gird himself, and make them to sit down to meat, and will come forth and serve them.
38 And if he shall come in the second watch, or come in the third watch, and find them so, blessed are those servants.
39 And this know, that if the goodman of the house had known what hour the thief would come, he would have watched, and not have suffered his house to be broken through.
40 Be ye therefore ready also: for the Son of man cometh at an hour when ye think not.

12.35-48. The Lord teaches His disciples to be vigilant particularly as it relates to His return to earth to set up His kingdom. He invites them to be like servants in a big household waiting for their Lord to return from a wedding (v36). They are clothed and ready (figurative meaning of 'loins girded' v35) with lamps in their hands to receive him even although it is dark ('lights burning' v35). It does not matter what time of night the Master comes they are ready (v38). They will not be found sleeping (v39-40).

12.39 'Goodman' – owner of the house.

The Parable of the Steward

41 Then Peter said unto him, Lord, speakest thou this parable unto us, or even to all?
42 And the Lord said, Who then is that faithful and wise steward, whom his lord shall make ruler over his household, to give them their portion of meat in due season?

12.40 Peter responded to the Lord's teaching wondering if this teaching applied to the disciples as well as everyone else. This gave the Lord an opportunity to use a parable (parable of the householder v42-48) to illustrate the importance of readiness and living in the light of the return of Christ.

12.42 – all disciples are stewards

who have been entrusted with the Lord's truths, gifts, and opportunities to serve His people in the days of His absence.

12.43-44 Rewards will be given for faithful service when the Lord Jesus returns.

12.45-46 Those who claim to be stewards and begin to maltreat God's people are showing that they are counterfeit and really unbelievers. They will be judged severely when the Lord returns. 'in sunder' means 'in pieces'.

12.47-48 Those who are believers but whose service has not been according to the will of the Lord will suffer loss. Not all will suffer the same loss – greater responsibility will bring greater judgment.

12.49-59. The Lord proceeds to show that allegiance to Christ will bring persecution. His teaching and healing ministry would soon end. He was going to the cross to die. His life and death brought division. He anticipates the fire of Calvary being lit already (v49). He had a baptism to undergo which is figurative of His death on Calvary's cross. Nothing could thwart His purpose to go there and die for the sins of the world. He would not be 'straightened' i.e. hemmed in (v50). His demands would bring division in families (v51-53), those who love Him and those who hate Him. He challenges the people that if they can anticipate the weather through observation of clouds (v54-56), why cannot the events around them allow them to make a proper and righteous assessment of His claims. The Lord called them hypocrites. If

43 Blessed is that servant, whom his lord when he cometh shall find so doing.

44 Of a truth I say unto you, that he will make him ruler over all that he hath.

45 But and if that servant say in his heart, My lord delayeth his coming; and shall begin to beat the menservants and maidens, and to eat and drink, and to be drunken;

46 The lord of that servant will come in a day when he looketh not for him, and at an hour when he is not aware, and will cut him in sunder, and will appoint him his portion with the unbelievers.

47 And that servant, which knew his lord's will, and prepared not himself, neither did according to his will, shall be beaten with many stripes.

48 But he that knew not, and did commit things worthy of stripes, shall be beaten with few stripes. For unto whomsoever much is given, of him shall be much required: and to whom men have committed much, of him they will ask the more.

Christ as the Divider of Men

49 I am come to send fire on the earth; and what will I, if it be already kindled?

50 But I have a baptism to be baptized with; and how am I straitened till it be accomplished!

51 Suppose ye that I am come to give peace on earth? I tell you, Nay; but rather division:

52 For from henceforth there shall be five in one house divided, three against two, and two against three.

53 The father shall be divided against the son, and the son against the father; the mother against the daughter, and the daughter against the mother; the mother in law against her daughter in law, and the daughter in law against her mother in law.

Discerning the Time

54 And he said also to the people, When ye see a cloud rise out of the west, straightway ye say, There cometh a shower; and so it is.

55 And when ye see the south wind blow, ye say, There will be heat; and it cometh to pass.

56 Ye hypocrites, ye can discern the face of the sky

and of the earth; but how is it that ye do not discern
this time?
57 Yea, and why even of yourselves judge ye not
what is right?

The Last Mite Paid

58 When thou goest with thine adversary to the
magistrate, as thou art in the way, give diligence
that thou mayest be delivered from him; lest he
hale thee to the judge, and the judge deliver thee
to the officer, and the officer cast thee into prison.
59 I tell thee, thou shalt not depart thence, till thou
hast paid the very last mite.

they were being taken to court by someone they would try and sort the claim out of court if possible (v58). He warned that they did not have long to settle their claim with Christ, and they should not allow their relationship with Christ to end up in that final court of God. The solemn warning is that they would pay the full price (v59)!

Reflective Questions and Notes

A. What did the Lord mean in verse 15?

B. What tragic mistake did the rich fool make? v16-21

C. What was the Lord illustrating from the birds, flowers and grass? v22-32

D. What did the Lord mean in v50?

E. What is the main lesson of the parable of servants waiting for their lord from the wedding, the parable of the householder, and the illustration from wind and clouds? v35-56

Luke 13

Except Ye Repent

1 There were present at that season some that told him of the Galilaeans, whose blood Pilate had mingled with their sacrifices.

2 And Jesus answering said unto them, Suppose ye that these Galilaeans were sinners above all the Galilaeans, because they suffered such things?

3 I tell you, Nay: but, except ye repent, ye shall all likewise perish.

4 Or those eighteen, upon whom the tower in Siloam fell, and slew them, think ye that they were sinners above all men that dwelt in Jerusalem?

5 I tell you, Nay: but, except ye repent, ye shall all likewise perish.

The Parable of the Fig Tree in the Vineyard

6 He spake also this parable; A certain man had a fig tree planted in his vineyard; and he came and sought fruit thereon, and found none.

7 Then said he unto the dresser of his vineyard, Behold, these three years I come seeking fruit on this fig tree, and find none: cut it down; why cumbereth it the ground?

8 And he answering said unto him, Lord, let it alone this year also, till I shall dig about it, and dung it:

9 And if it bear fruit, well: and if not, then after that thou shalt cut it down.

The Woman Healed on the Sabbath

10 And he was teaching in one of the synagogues on the sabbath.

11 And, behold, there was a woman which had a spirit of infirmity eighteen years, and was bowed together, and could in no wise lift up herself.

12 And when Jesus saw her, he called her to him, and said unto her, Woman, thou art loosed from thine infirmity.

13 And he laid his hands on her: and immediately she was made straight, and glorified God.

14 And the ruler of the synagogue answered with indignation, because that Jesus had healed on the sabbath day, and said unto the people, There are six days in which men ought to work: in them therefore come and be healed, and not on the sabbath day.

Chapter 13 Repentance and Reality

13.1 The Lord hears of the barbaric killing Pilate did to Galileans for political purposes. The Lord uses this as an opportunity to warn the people of the need to repent of sins.

13.2-5 He invites them to consider whether these Galileans, or those who died at the recent tragedy where a wall fell over in Siloam, were the worst of sinners? No - of course not. He stresses that all of us are in the same place, not just some of us. Except we repent of our sins we will all perish – but this time at the hands of God.

13.6-8 The Lord's parable of the fig tree illustrates that God is caring for us despite our unfaithfulness, providing for us even if we do not produce any fruit for Him. However, if this fruitless life persists we will eventually be cut down just like a dead fig tree. Israel is pictured as a dead fig tree despite all the loving attention from the Father.

13.10-17 The healing of the woman who was bent over for eighteen years. This miracle happened on a sabbath day and the response by the ruler of the synagogue illustrates this fruitless life. The Lord made her straight again and she immediately gave God the glory. The ruler of the synagogue was unhappy and instead of rejoicing and thanking God he objected to this being done on the sabbath day (a Saturday). The Lord called him a hypocrite and invited him to think what he would do if one of his cattle or donkeys fell into a ditch on the sabbath day.

Surely the lady is better than his cattle. She had known healing after being crippled for 18 years. This exposure of hypocrisy was understood by all the people who observed.

15 The Lord then answered him, and said, Thou
hypocrite, doth not each one of you on the sabbath
loose his ox or his ass from the stall, and lead him
away to watering?
16 And ought not this woman, being a daughter
of Abraham, whom Satan hath bound, lo, these
eighteen years, be loosed from this bond on the
sabbath day?
17 And when he had said these things, all his
adversaries were ashamed: and all the people
rejoiced for all the glorious things that were done
by him.

13.18-21 This hypocrisy is highlighted further by two short parables. The mustard seed tree can grow to 3 or 4m in height. It has branches which birds sit on. So, the kingdom of God is really growing from the seed of the Word of God but there are those who claim to be part of it (like the birds) who have never come from the seed of God's word. The leaven (yeast) in the meal is a picture of the evil and pride of the Pharisees being a baneful influence on the kingdom of God.
13.22-30 The Lord taught the importance of being real and authentic and of being in earnest about salvation and going through the narrow gate to receive eternal life. The day of opportunity to be saved will soon be past (v22-24). He told the parable of the Master of a household who will one day shut the door of his house (v25). He does not know those who then come knocking after the door is shut, and they hear the tragic words 'depart' (v27). They had not wanted Him in the past and now it is too late. They have missed the kingdom. Others will be there from all over the world (v29) including the faithful of the past (e.g. Abraham v28) but they won't be there, not because they

Parables of the Mustard Seed and the Leaven

18 Then said he, Unto what is the kingdom of God
like? and whereunto shall I resemble it?
19 It is like a grain of mustard seed, which a man
took, and cast into his garden; and it grew, and
waxed a great tree; and the fowls of the air lodged
in the branches of it.
20 And again he said, Whereunto shall I liken the
kingdom of God?
21 It is like leaven, which a woman took and hid in
three measures of meal, till the whole was leavened.

Are There Few that be Saved?

22 And he went through the cities and villages,
teaching, and journeying toward Jerusalem.
23 Then said one unto him, Lord, are there few that
be saved? And he said unto them,
24 Strive to enter in at the strait gate: for many, I say
unto you, will seek to enter in, and shall not be able.
25 When once the master of the house is risen up,
and hath shut to the door, and ye begin to stand
without, and to knock at the door, saying, Lord, Lord,
open unto us; and he shall answer and say unto you,
I know you not whence ye are:
26 Then shall ye begin to say, We have eaten and
drunk in thy presence, and thou hast taught in our
streets.
27 But he shall say, I tell you, I know you not whence
ye are; depart from me, all ye workers of iniquity.
28 There shall be weeping and gnashing of teeth,
when ye shall see Abraham, and Isaac, and Jacob,

and all the prophets, in the kingdom of God, and
you yourselves thrust out.
29 And they shall come from the east, and from the
west, and from the north, and from the south, and
shall sit down in the kingdom of God.
30 And, behold, there are last which shall be first,
and there are first which shall be last.

Herod, that Fox

31 The same day there came certain of the Pharisees,
saying unto him, Get thee out, and depart hence:
for Herod will kill thee.
32 And he said unto them, Go ye, and tell that fox,
Behold, I cast out devils, and I do cures to day and
to morrow, and the third day I shall be perfected.
33 Nevertheless I must walk to day, and to morrow,
and the day following: for it cannot be that a prophet
perish out of Jerusalem.

O Jerusalem, Jerusalem!

34 O Jerusalem, Jerusalem, which killest the
prophets, and stonest them that are sent unto
thee; how often would I have gathered thy children
together, as a hen doth gather her brood under her
wings, and ye would not!
35 Behold, your house is left unto you desolate:
and verily I say unto you, Ye shall not see me, until
the time come when ye shall say, Blessed is he that
cometh in the name of the Lord.

were not cared for, or there was no opportunity but because they did not repent and accept God's salvation

13.30-33 The teaching of the Lord is too much for the Pharisees and so they warn Him of Herod's intention to kill Him. The Lord replies by saying that no one can stop Him carrying out His purpose. Intriguingly, He speaks of three days of service and of the 'third day' – a likely reference to His resurrection.

13.34 -35. The Lord cries out in love and sorrow to Jerusalem for their obstinate unwillingness to repent, likening Himself to a hen that would want to have gathered them like chicks to a place of protection. As a result of their unwillingness. judgment will surely follow until, as Psalm 118.26 says, Israel acknowledge He is Messiah and say, 'Blessed is He that comes in the Name of the Lord'. This anticipates the day of the national repentance of Israel.

Reflective Questions and Notes

A. What was the big lesson the Lord brought out from the barbaric killing by Pilate or the man made disaster in the badly erected wall? v1-5

B. What is the main lesson of the parable of the fig tree? v6-9

C. What is the main lesson of the illustration of the householder? v23-30

D. Who is the fox? v32

E. What does the illustration of the hen tell us about Christ? v34 What does it tell us about unrepentant hearts?

Luke 14

The Challenge to Pharisees and Scribes

1 And it came to pass, as he went into the house of one of the chief Pharisees to eat bread on the sabbath day, that they watched him.

2 And, behold, there was a certain man before him which had the dropsy.

3 And Jesus answering spake unto the lawyers and Pharisees, saying, Is it lawful to heal on the sabbath day?

4 And they held their peace. And he took him, and healed him, and let him go;

5 And answered them, saying, Which of you shall have an ass or an ox fallen into a pit, and will not straightway pull him out on the sabbath day?

6 And they could not answer him again to these things.

Taking the Lowest Room

7 And he put forth a parable to those which were bidden, when he marked how they chose out the chief rooms; saying unto them.

8 When thou art bidden of any man to a wedding, sit not down in the highest room; lest a more honourable man than thou be bidden of him;

9 And he that bade thee and him come and say to thee, Give this man place; and thou begin with shame to take the lowest room.

10 But when thou art bidden, go and sit down in the lowest room; that when he that bade thee cometh, he may say unto thee, Friend, go up higher: then shalt thou have worship in the presence of them that sit at meat with thee.

11 For whosoever exalteth himself shall be abased; and he that humbleth himself shall be exalted.

12 Then said he also to him that bade him, When thou makest a dinner or a supper, call not thy friends, nor thy brethren, neither thy kinsmen, nor thy rich neighbours; lest they also bid thee again, and a recompence be made thee.

13 But when thou makest a feast, call the poor, the maimed, the lame, the blind:

14 And thou shalt be blessed; for they cannot recompense thee: for thou shalt be recompensed at the resurrection of the just.

Chapter 14: Self Denial.

4.1 The Lord's life was constantly scrutinised. This whole episode may have been a planned trap by the Pharisees.

14.2 'dropsy' – excess fluid building in soft tissue in the body. It is normally called edema today, which is caused by congestive heart failure.

14.3-4 The Pharisees were dominated by legal rules of their own making, There is no compassion for the man or even wonder that such illnesses could be cured by Christ.

14.5-6 The Lord enquired if they would apply such teaching to their animals? The proud Pharisee had no answer.

14.7-11 The Lord told a parable about humility and of a man invited to a wedding. He said that the man should not try and assume he was one of the most important guests by taking a seat near the bridal party but rather he should take the lowest place. Those that put themselves up will be put down and those who lower themselves will be exalted. God blesses humility.

14.12-15 The Lord says to those who have invited Him to dinner that we should try and invite people who cannot ever repay us – the poor, disabled ('maimed'), lame and blind. The reward will not be immediate but eternal (v14). God blesses compassion.

14.15 A man who ate with Him begins to think of the blessing of eating bread in the kingdom of God.

14.16-27 The Lord responded by telling a parable of a man who made a great celebratory feast. This parable will speak of those who will eat in the kingdom of God. Those who had previously been invited and initially responded as coming ('were bidden') are summoned to come on the day of the feast, by a special messenger (v17). Then the excuses start. One is affected by his long-term investments (land v18), another with intermediate financial assets (oxen) and what they produce annually (v19). Finally, another is more interested in his immediate domestic affairs (his wife – v20). The man that was holding the feast was angry at their refusal to come and filled his house with people who were poor, disabled, crippled and blind (v21). He made sure the feast was full by going out of his way to find people who were homeless and living in rural poverty encouraging them all to come (v22-23). Those who were initially invited but refused would not be part of the feast he had prepared (v24). He explains the parable partly by making it clear that heaven will be full of those that receive the invitation to 'come to Christ' and love Christ more than any natural relationship or ambition. Indeed, in comparison to love for Him all other relationships should be classified as 'hate' (v25-26). Discipleship demands complete sacrifice (v27).

14.28 The Lord underscores this teaching with two illustrations. The first illustration is a man who builds a tower but has not done the calculations of the cost and cannot complete it (v28-30). Discipleship for Christ is costly and will cost everything not just part of your life. The second illustration (v31-32) is a king who is about to attack another king and ponders whether he has the human resources to be successful. He is outnumbered and considers whether he

The Great Gospel Supper

15 And when one of them that sat at meat with him
heard these things, he said unto him, Blessed is he
that shall eat bread in the kingdom of God.
16 Then said he unto him, A certain man made a
great supper, and bade many:
17 And sent his servant at supper time to say to them
that were bidden, Come; for all things are now ready.
18 And they all with one consent began to make
excuse. The first said unto him, I have bought a
piece of ground, and I must needs go and see it: I
pray thee have me excused.
19 And another said, I have bought five yoke of oxen,
and I go to prove them: I pray thee have me excused.
20 And another said, I have married a wife, and
therefore I cannot come.
21 So that servant came, and shewed his lord these
things. Then the master of the house being angry
said to his servant, Go out quickly into the streets
and lanes of the city, and bring in hither the poor,
and the maimed, and the halt, and the blind.
22 And the servant said, Lord, it is done as thou hast
commanded, and yet there is room.
23 And the lord said unto the servant, Go out into
the highways and hedges, and compel them to come
in, that my house may be filled.
24 For I say unto you, That none of those men which
were bidden shall taste of my supper.

Bearing the Cross

25 And there went great multitudes with him: and
he turned, and said unto them,
26 If any man come to me, and hate not his father,
and mother, and wife, and children, and brethren,
and sisters, yea, and his own life also, he cannot be
my disciple.
27 And whosoever doth not bear his cross, and come
after me, cannot be my disciple.

Parables of the Tower, the King and the Tasteless Salt

28 For which of you, intending to build a tower,
sitteth not down first, and counteth the cost,
whether he have sufficient to finish it?

29 Lest haply, after he hath laid the foundation,
and is not able to finish it, all that behold it begin
to mock him,
30 Saying, This man began to build, and was not
able to finish.
31 Or what king, going to make war against another
king, sitteth not down first, and consulteth whether
he be able with ten thousand to meet him that
cometh against him with twenty thousand?
32 Or else, while the other is yet a great way off,
he sendeth an ambassage, and desireth conditions
of peace.
33 So likewise, whosoever he be of you that
forsaketh not all that he hath, he cannot be my
disciple.
34 Salt is good: but if the salt have lost his savour,
wherewith shall it be seasoned?
35 It is neither fit for the land, nor yet for the
dunghill; but men cast it out. He that hath ears to
hear, let him hear.

should he risk going to war and forsake all or send ahead ambassadors (ambassage – v32) and negotiate a peace pact? The Lord says when it comes to His discipleship it requires the key decision to forsake all (v33). He said those that try to be His disciples but love self, place, power and their wealth are like salt that has lost its taste. It is useless for meals, for changing the acidity/ alkalinity of soil, even for destroying vegetation due to its antibacterial qualities (dung hill). Men throw it away. God cannot use such people as they are full of their own self-importance.

Reflective Questions and Notes

A. Self-importance and religious pride can crush out compassion for those in need. How did the Lord illustrate this? v1-6

B. What did the Lord say about our conduct when invited for a meal and our approach when inviting others to a meal? Why? v7-14

C. How did the Lord answer the question or statement of verse 15? Who is it that will eat bread in the kingdom of God? v16-27

D. What is the Lord teaching in the stories of the tower, army and salt? v28-35

Luke 15

The Great Trilogy

1 Then drew near unto him all the publicans and
sinners for to hear him.
2 And the Pharisees and scribes murmured, saying,
This man receiveth sinners, and eateth with them.
3 And he spake this parable unto them, saying,
4 What man of you, having an hundred sheep, if
he lose one of them, doth not leave the ninety and
nine in the wilderness, and go after that which is
lost, until he find it?
5 And when he hath found it, he layeth it on his
shoulders, rejoicing.
6 And when he cometh home, he calleth together his
friends and neighbours, saying unto them, Rejoice
with me; for I have found my sheep which was lost.
7 I say unto you, that likewise joy shall be in
heaven over one sinner that repenteth, more than
over ninety and nine just persons, which need no
repentance.
8 Either what woman having ten pieces of silver,
if she lose one piece, doth not light a candle, and
sweep the house, and seek diligently till she find it?
9 And when she hath found it, she calleth her friends
and her neighbours together, saying, Rejoice with
me; for I have found the piece which I had lost.
10 Likewise, I say unto you, there is joy in the presence
of the angels of God over one sinner that repenteth.
11 And he said, A certain man had two sons:
12 And the younger of them said to his father,
Father, give me the portion of goods that falleth to
me. And he divided unto them his living.
13 And not many days after the younger son
gathered all together, and took his journey into a
far country, and there wasted his substance with
riotous living.
14 And when he had spent all, there arose a mighty
famine in that land; and he began to be in want.
15 And he went and joined himself to a citizen of
that country; and he sent him into his fields to feed
swine.

15.1-32 The Love of God for those who are lost.

This whole chapter is about us knowing that we are lost and the love of God going out to us, to find us, and bring us to a place of safety. The parables are given when the Pharisees had criticised Him for receiving certain people, who they considered below them (v2). There is a danger that we think we are not lost.

15.3 This is one parable in 3 stories: lost sheep, lost silver, lost son.

15.4-7. Lost sheep.

The joy of the Lord Jesus and all the angels when one sinner repents is compared to a good shepherd rejoicing after going after one sheep until he finds it. He lays it on his shoulders crying out to all his friends 'rejoice with me'. The 99 sheep represent the Pharisees (and those like them) who think they do not need to repent.

15.8-10 Lost silver coin.

The joy of angels when a sinner repents of their sins is likened to a woman rejoicing who after searching her house from top to bottom finds the missing silver coin. In both pictures the value of the sinner to the Lord is seen in the value of the silver to the woman or the sheep to the shepherd. The extent to which God is seeking the sinner for salvation is seen in the long-distance search by the shepherd and the diligent search of the house by the woman.

15.11-32. The Lost Son.

The younger son requests his inheritance before his father dies. Both sons are given it (v12). The older son would get the double portion. The younger son squanders it with his excessive hedonistic lifestyle (v13) and he was in 'want' (v14-means 'need') and he would 'fain' (v16 -means 'desire to') actually eat what the pigs ate.

15.17- 19 It is when he is at rock bottom that he becomes authentic and realises his sin against God and against his father. The sinner repenting before God is pictured in the younger son repenting and confessing his sin to God and his father.

15.20-24 The joy of God the Father in forgiving a sinner is seen in the Father running to his son, hugging, kissing (v20), clothing (v22) and celebrating his return (v23-24).

15.25-32 The response by the older son represent the self-deception of the Pharisees. The older son thinks he is much more important than the younger son, the way he speaks to his father is rude and he stays outside the house, outside of the warmth of the Father's love. The younger son was selfish but older son is self-righteous. The younger son's besetting sin was lust, the older son's besetting sin is pride. The younger son forsakes self and repents. The older son is angry. The younger son says, 'Father, I have sinned' casting himself on the father's love and care, the older son questions the father's care saying, 'You never gave me'. The younger son was lost and is now found, was blind and is now

16 And he would fain have filled his belly with the
husks that the swine did eat: and no man gave
unto him.
17 And when he came to himself, he said, How many
hired servants of my father's have bread enough and
to spare, and I perish with hunger!
18 I will arise and go to my father, and will say unto
him, Father, I have sinned against heaven, and
before thee,
19 And am no more worthy to be called thy son:
make me as one of thy hired servants.
20 And he arose, and came to his father. But when
he was yet a great way off, his father saw him, and
had compassion, and ran, and fell on his neck, and
kissed him.
21 And the son said unto him, Father, I have sinned
against heaven, and in thy sight, and am no more
worthy to be called thy son.
22 But the father said to his servants, Bring forth
the best robe, and put it on him; and put a ring on
his hand, and shoes on his feet:
23 And bring hither the fatted calf, and kill it; and
let us eat, and be merry:
24 For this my son was dead, and is alive again; he
was lost, and is found. And they began to be merry.
25 Now his elder son was in the field: and as he
came and drew nigh to the house, he heard musick
and dancing.
26 And he called one of the servants, and asked
what these things meant.
27 And he said unto him, Thy brother is come; and
thy father hath killed the fatted calf, because he
hath received him safe and sound.
28 And he was angry, and would not go in: therefore
came his father out, and intreated him.
29 And he answering said to his father, Lo, these many
years do I serve thee, neither transgressed I at any
time thy commandment: and yet thou never gavest
me a kid, that I might make merry with my friends:
30 But as soon as this thy son was come, which hath
devoured thy living with harlots, thou hast killed for
him the fatted calf.

31 And he said unto him, Son, thou art ever with
me, and all that I have is thine.
32 It was meet that we should make merry, and
be glad: for this thy brother was dead, and is alive
again; and was lost, and is found.

seeing. The older son remains angry and unsaved. How solemn and sad.

15.1-32 The three pictures are also a picture of the Triune God seeking the sinner for salvation. The Shepherd is a picture of the Lord Jesus sacrificing His life for the sheep (John 10. 9). The woman seeking the silver is a picture of the diligent search of the Holy Spirit to convict of sin and righteousness and judgement (John 16. 8). The father running to seek his son is a picture of God the Father ready to receive the repentant sinner.

Reflective Questions and Notes

A. What is the main lesson from all three stories of the lost sheep, coin and son?

B. What is the rejoicing of the shepherd with his lost sheep on his shoulders or the women with her lost coin in her hand likened to? v7-8; v9-10

C. What was the young son's big problem? How was it resolved? v11-32

D. What was the older son's big problem? Was it ever solved? v11-32

Luke 16

How Much Owest Thou unto my Lord?

1 And he said also unto his disciples, There was a
certain rich man, which had a steward; and the same
was accused unto him that he had wasted his goods.
2 And he called him, and said unto him, How is
it that I hear this of thee? give an account of thy
stewardship; for thou mayest be no longer steward.
3 Then the steward said within himself, What
shall I do? for my lord taketh away from me the
stewardship: I cannot dig; to beg I am ashamed.
4 I am resolved what to do, that, when I am put out
of the stewardship, they may receive me into their
houses.
5 So he called every one of his lord's debtors unto
him, and said unto the first, How much owest thou
unto my lord?
6 And he said, An hundred measures of oil. And he
said unto him, Take thy bill, and sit down quickly,
and write fifty.
7 Then said he to another, And how much owest
thou? And he said, An hundred measures of wheat.
And he said unto him, Take thy bill, and write
fourscore.
8 And the lord commended the unjust steward,
because he had done wisely: for the children of
this world are in their generation wiser than the
children of light.
9 And I say unto you, Make to yourselves friends of
the mammon of unrighteousness; that, when ye fail,
they may receive you into everlasting habitations.
10 He that is faithful in that which is least is faithful
also in much: and he that is unjust in the least is
unjust also in much.
11 If therefore ye have not been faithful in the
unrighteous mammon, who will commit to your
trust the true riches?
12 And if ye have not been faithful in that which
is another man's, who shall give you that which is
your own?
13 No servant can serve two masters: for either he

Chapter 16 Stewardship and Eternity

16.1-13 The parable of the unjust steward.

The Lord taught this parable to bring out the foresight of the steward. He was about to be removed from his post as a steward and began to think ahead (v2-3). He helped some debtors by reducing their debt (v5-7) and helped the rich man realise some of his credit, for which he was grateful (v8). The Lord's main teaching point from the parable is not to follow the methods of the man, but to follow his foresight. We can turn material things into a spiritual and eternal use (v9). We need to look ahead and consider a day when we will be in need or die and go to heaven ('when ye fail' v9). The good deeds done to others when we had plenty money ('mammon of unrighteousness') and opportunity to help others ('make to yourselves friends') will return in an eternal way later ('everlasting habitations' v9). This is true both in this life and specifically of heaven in the next. The Lord also taught that as disciples of Christ those who are faithful and righteous in the small things in life are also faithful and righteous in the big matters (v10). Also, if we are not good stewards of the money and material things that God has given us how can we expect the Lord to commit to us riches of a greater and eternal value (v11)? We cannot serve two masters – it is either serving God or serving riches, not both (v13).

16.14-18 This teaching on proper stewardship of money led to ridicule from the covetous Pharisee (v14). This brought about the Lord's condemnation (v15) and a reminder that discipleship brings sacrifice. In the present phase of the kingdom of God we must be in earnest if we want to enter it (v16). The standards are high and uncompromising (v17).

These demands on being faithful in monetary matters also apply to marital matters (v18).

16.19-31 The rich man and Lazarus.
At this point the Lord illustrates His teaching with a real story. The rich man in the story is selfish and self-centred and not interested in the poor man Lazarus (whose name means 'helped of God') at his gate. However, in eternity (after death) the poor man who depended upon God went to heaven (called Abraham's bosom' v22), the rich man who thought only of this life went to hell (v23). The attitude of the rich selfish man is different now – longing for some relief from the pain (v24). He is reminded that he had opportunity to be kind to Lazarus in life and chose not to and he had opportunity to be a steward of what God had given him in life and chose not to (v25). Now there was no possibility of changing this (v26). The rich man

will hate the one, and love the other; or else he will hold to the one, and despise the other. Ye cannot serve God and mammon.

The Contrast between Divine and Human Estimation

14 And the Pharisees also, who were covetous, heard
all these things: and they derided him.
15 And he said unto them, Ye are they which justify
yourselves before men; but God knoweth your
hearts: for that which is highly esteemed among
men is abomination in the sight of God.
16 The law and the prophets were until John: since
that time the kingdom of God is preached, and every
man presseth into it.
17 And it is easier for heaven and earth to pass, than
one tittle of the law to fail.

Divorce and Adultery

18 Whosoever putteth away his wife, and marrieth
another, committeth adultery: and whosoever
marrieth her that is put away from her husband
committeth adultery.

Two Men in Time and in Eternity

19 There was a certain rich man, which was clothed
in purple and fine linen, and fared sumptuously
every day:
20 And there was a certain beggar named Lazarus,
which was laid at his gate, full of sores,
21 And desiring to be fed with the crumbs which
fell from the rich man's table: moreover the dogs
came and licked his sores.
22 And it came to pass, that the beggar died, and
was carried by the angels into Abraham's bosom:
the rich man also died, and was buried;
23 And in hell he lift up his eyes, being in torments,
and seeth Abraham afar off, and Lazarus in his
bosom.
24 And he cried and said, Father Abraham, have
mercy on me, and send Lazarus, that he may dip
the tip of his finger in water, and cool my tongue;
for I am tormented in this flame.
25 But Abraham said, Son, remember that thou in
thy lifetime receivedst thy good things, and likewise

Lazarus evil things: but now he is comforted, and
thou art tormented.
26 And beside all this, between us and you there
is a great gulf fixed: so that they which would pass
from hence to you cannot; neither can they pass to
us, that would come from thence.
27 Then he said, I pray thee therefore, father, that
thou wouldest send him to my father's house:
28 For I have five brethren; that he may testify unto
them, lest they also come into this place of torment.
29 Abraham saith unto him, They have Moses and
the prophets; let them hear them.
30 And he said, Nay, father Abraham: but if one went
unto them from the dead, they will repent.
31 And he said unto him, If they hear not Moses
and the prophets, neither will they be persuaded,
though one rose from the dead.

longs that people would be sent to tell his brothers about hell (v28). Interestingly, Abraham says that the Bible ('Moses and the prophets') already warns of hell. If they won't hear God speaking (the Word of God) it would not matter if they heard another human - even if that human had already been dead (v29-31).

In the light of these eternal realities, which world are we living for?

Reflective Questions and Notes

A. What is the main lesson from the parable of the unjust steward? v1-13

B. Why did the Pharisees reject this parable? v14-15

C. What was the rich man's main fault? What were the consequences? v16-26

D. Whose word is even more important and powerful than the voice of a dead man brought back to life? v27-31

Luke 17

Trespass and Forgiveness

1 Then said he unto the disciples, It is impossible but that offences will come: but woe unto him, through whom they come!

2 It were better for him that a millstone were hanged about his neck, and he cast into the sea, than that he should offend one of these little ones.

3 Take heed to yourselves: If thy brother trespass against thee, rebuke him; and if he repent, forgive him.

4 And if he trespass against thee seven times in a day, and seven times in a day turn again to thee, saying, I repent; thou shalt forgive him.

The Smallness of Faith

5 And the apostles said unto the Lord, Increase our faith.

6 And the Lord said, If ye had faith as a grain of mustard seed, ye might say unto this sycamine tree, Be thou plucked up by the root, and be thou planted in the sea; and it should obey you.

The Duty of Servants

7 But which of you, having a servant plowing or feeding cattle, will say unto him by and by, when he is come from the field, Go and sit down to meat?

8 And will not rather say unto him, Make ready wherewith I may sup, and gird thyself, and serve me, till I have eaten and drunken; and afterward thou shalt eat and drink?

9 Doth he thank that servant because he did the things that were commanded him? I trow not.

10 So likewise ye, when ye shall have done all those things which are commanded you, say, We are unprofitable servants: we have done that which was our duty to do.

Where are the Nine?

11 And it came to pass, as he went to Jerusalem, that he passed through the midst of Samaria and Galilee.

12 And as he entered into a certain village, there met him ten men that were lepers, which stood afar off:

13 And they lifted up their voices, and said, Jesus, Master, have mercy on us.

Chapter 17 The importance of repentance and forgiveness.

17.1-4 The Lord teaches about the importance of not hurting or stumbling others, particularly children or young believers. He said those who stumble the little children would be better away to heaven (v2)! He moves on to discuss the matter of our willingness to forgive our brothers and sisters in Christ – even if it is seven times a day!

17.5-10 The apostles clearly feel that such forgiveness is almost impossible for them and so they ask for their faith to be increased (v5). The Lord tells them that even a little faith would allow them to remove trees never mind the small barriers to faith that they saw in His teaching about forgiving your brother (v6). He reminds them in v7-10 that at the end of the day a man who has employees such as household servants will expect them to make the meal at night. ('Trow' means 'think' v9). The lesson is clear (v10): instead of thinking you need bigger faith what you need to do is simply obey God's Word – forgive your brother no matter how many times he hurts you and repents. Forgiveness is the outcome of obedience to our Lord.

17.11-19. The cleansing of the ten lepers takes place in Samaria. The lepers were social outcasts who had to stand at a distance from others ('stood afar off'- v12). They all collectively cry to the Lord for mercy (v13). The Lord asks them to show themselves to the priests who had never seen anyone cured from leprosy. (Leviticus 13-14 gives details for the priests on this).

On the way they were all cleansed. Only one Samaritan came back to give thanks, but He still healed all ten. The Lord is illustrating that forgiveness extends to everyone - even Samaritans and lepers and mercy should be extended even when the person is unthankful. The person who was thankful, however, was made whole ('saved'). He received a greater blessing than his leprosy removed, but also God's salvation (v19).

17.20-37 Israel and the need for repentance.

The Pharisees asks questions about the coming of the kingdom of God (v20). The Lord initially shows them that the King is already here 'within you" or 'in your midst' (v20-21)- but they have not accepted Him. The Lord then speaks of the future kingdom when He, the Son of Man, will return to set up His kingdom. There will be no confusion about when He has returned, as great things will happen in the heavens (v23-24). But first He will be rejected by His own people – they will not repent (v25). Like Noah's day (Genesis 6-8) after a time to repent, people will carry on as if nothing will happen and judgment will follow (v26-27). Like Lot's day (Genesis 19-20) after a time to repent, people will continue to live their lives without God and judgment will follow (V28-29). This is what it will be like when the Lord returns to set up His kingdom (v30). In the day of His return there be no point in accumulating a lot of household stuff or thinking about your job ('in the field')

14 And when he saw them, he said unto them, Go
shew yourselves unto the priests. And it came to
pass, that, as they went, they were cleansed.
15 And one of them, when he saw that he was
healed, turned back, and with a loud voice glorified
God,
16 And fell down on his face at his feet, giving him
thanks: and he was a Samaritan.
17 And Jesus answering said, Were there not ten
cleansed? but where are the nine?
18 There are not found that returned to give glory
to God, save this stranger.
19 And he said unto him, Arise, go thy way: thy faith
hath made thee whole.

Two Aspects of the Kingdoms

20 And when he was demanded of the Pharisees,
when the kingdom of God should come, he
answered them and said, The kingdom of God
cometh not with observation:
21 Neither shall they say, Lo here! or, lo there! for,
behold, the kingdom of God is within you.
22 And he said unto the disciples, The days will
come, when ye shall desire to see one of the days
of the Son of man, and ye shall not see it.
23 And they shall say to you, See here; or, see there:
go not after them, nor follow them.
24 For as the lightning, that lighteneth out of the
one part under heaven, shineth unto the other
part under heaven; so shall also the Son of man be
in his day.
25 But first must he suffer many things, and be
rejected of this generation.
26 And as it was in the days of Noe, so shall it be
also in the days of the Son of man.
27 They did eat, they drank, they married wives,
they were given in marriage, until the day that
Noah entered into the ark, and the flood came, and
destroyed them all.
28 Likewise also as it was in the days of Lot; they
did eat, they drank, they bought, they sold, they
planted, they builded;
29 But the same day that Lot went out of Sodom

it rained fire and brimstone from heaven, and destroyed them all.
30 Even thus shall it be in the day when the Son of man is revealed.
31 In that day, he which shall be upon the housetop, and his stuff in the house, let him not come down to take it away: and he that is in the field, let him likewise not return back.
32 Remember Lot's wife.
33 Whosoever shall seek to save his life shall lose it; and whosoever shall lose his life shall preserve it.
34 I tell you, in that night there shall be two men in one bed; the one shall be taken, and the other shall be left.
35 Two women shall be grinding together; the one shall be taken, and the other left.
36 Two men shall be in the field; the one shall be taken, and the other left.
37 And they answered and said unto him, Where, Lord? And he said unto them, Wheresoever the body is, thither will the eagles be gathered together.

(v31). Lot's wife looked back with desire for these things in the day of judgment (v32) and was judged (Gen 19. 26). Those who try to save their old way of life will lose it. Those who give away their old way of life and embrace Christ will find life (v34). When the Lord comes He will divide those who have repented and accepted His forgiveness from those who are not repentant (v34-36). The disciples wanted to know where the Lord Jesus was coming to . He told them that this would not be a mystery. As they knew where a dead carcase was whenever they saw eagles and vultures circling around, so they all will know where the Lord Jesus is coming to whenever they see the armies of this world circle around and congregate at a particular place (v37). We know this to be Jerusalem and Armageddon from Revelation chapters 16-20.

Reflective Questions and Notes

A. Why did the disciples say, 'increase our faith'? v5

B. How many lepers cried for mercy? How many were cleansed? How many returned to say 'Thank You'? v11-19

C. What did the Lord mean when He said that 'the kingdom of God is in your midst'? v21

D. What will be the features of the human race prior to the return of Christ? v20-37

Luke 18

The Unjust judge and the justice of God

1 And he spake a parable unto them to this end, that
men ought always to pray, and not to faint;
2 Saying, There was in a city a judge, which feared
not God, neither regarded man:
3 And there was a widow in that city; and she came
unto him, saying, Avenge me of mine adversary.
4 And he would not for a while: but afterward he
said within himself, Though I fear not God, nor
regard man;
5 Yet because this widow troubleth me, I will avenge
her, lest by her continual coming she weary me.
6 And the Lord said, Hear what the unjust judge
saith.
7 And shall not God avenge his own elect, which
cry day and night unto him, though he bear long
with them?
8 I tell you that he will avenge them speedily.
Nevertheless when the Son of man cometh, shall
he find faith on the earth?

The Parable of the Pharisee and the Publican

9 And he spake this parable unto certain which
trusted in themselves that they were righteous, and
despised others:
10 Two men went up into the temple to pray; the
one a Pharisee, and the other a publican.
11 The Pharisee stood and prayed thus with himself,
God, I thank thee, that I am not as other men are,
extortioners, unjust, adulterers, or even as this
publican.
12 I fast twice in the week, I give tithes of all that
I possess.
13 And the publican, standing afar off, would not lift
up so much as his eyes unto heaven, but smote upon
his breast, saying, God be merciful to me a sinner.
14 I tell you, this man went down to his house
justified rather than the other: for every one that
exalteth himself shall be abased; and he that
humbleth himself shall be exalted.

The Lesson from a Little Child

15 And they brought unto him also infants, that he

Chapter 18 On the way to Jerusalem - reality in prayer

18.1-8 Parable of the unjust judge.

Having spoken about how the Lord will know the real from the unreal at His return (Ch 17), the Lord now turns to the reality of our prayer life and whether He would find any faithful when He returns (v8).The main lesson from the story of the widow women was the persistence she had in coming to the Judge for her adversary to be 'avenged' (i.e. for her to get justice- v3) which eventually worked. If this is true of an unjust judge how much truer it is of the only just Judge. When His people ('elect' v7) cry to Him in genuine prayer He hears speedily. How real is our prayer life? Do we pray in faith, in His will believing that God will answer our prayers?

18.9-14 The parable of the Pharisee and the Publican (tax collector).

As chapter 17 ended with two being divided at His return, so two are divided here in His presence. The reality of their prayer life is really brought home in no uncertain terms. The pride of the Pharisee is unbearable to hear as he seeks to tell God abut all his accomplishments (v11-12). The repentance of the tax collector is refreshing with his short seven-word prayer. He asks for mercy ((literally 'be propitious' – v13). This reminds us of the purpose of the death of Christ to appease or propitiate the wrath of God so that sins could be forgiven righteously. The tax collector is justified (i.e. declared righteous). The Pharisee was not.

18.15-18 The children brought

to the Lord.
The disciples tried to stop the children coming to Christ and were rebuked for it (v15). Children have no ego. They are real and genuine. This is the spirit of all serious enquirers to Christ – come as a child if you are to receive the kingdom (v16-17).

18.18-27 The rich young ruler. The ruler standing by thinks he can come to Christ without being a child. He wants to do something for eternal life. The Lord challenges him on his understanding of 'good' (v18). He initially instructs him to keep the ten commandments which the man affirms he has always kept (v19-20). This shows the man has never know the reality of the conviction of sin. The Lord challenges him on commandment number 10 (do not covet) and he fails and leaves Christ dejected (v22-23). The Lord Jesus is moved with compassion (v24), the riches of the man are more important to him than the reality of eternal life. The Lord says it is easier for a camel to go through a needle's eye than for a rich man to be saved (v25-26). This leads to the question 'Who then can be saved' (v26)? The reply about God's omnipotence is sublime (v27).

18.28-30 The reality of blessing for sacrifice for Christ.
Peter wonders what happens to those who have left all for Christ (as they had). The answer is blessing in this life and everlasting life in the next. God is no man's debtor.

would touch them: but when his disciples saw it, they rebuked them.
16 But Jesus called them unto him, and said, Suffer little children to come unto me, and forbid them not: for of such is the kingdom of God.
17 Verily I say unto you, Whosoever shall not receive the kingdom of God as a little child shall in no wise enter therein.

A Rich Young Ruler

18 And a certain ruler asked him, saying, Good Master, what shall I do to inherit eternal life?
19 And Jesus said unto him, Why callest thou me good? none is good, save one, that is, God.
20 Thou knowest the commandments, Do not commit adultery, Do not kill, Do not steal, Do not bear false witness, Honour thy father and thy mother.
21 And he said, All these have I kept from my youth up.
22 Now when Jesus heard these things, he said unto him, Yet lackest thou one thing: sell all that thou hast, and distribute unto the poor, and thou shalt have treasure in heaven: and come, follow me.
23 And when he heard this, he was very sorrowful: for he was very rich.
24 And when Jesus saw that he was very sorrowful, he said, How hardly shall they that have riches enter into the kingdom of God!
25 For it is easier for a camel to go through a needle's eye, than for a rich man to enter into the kingdom of God.
26 And they that heard it said, Who then can be saved?
27 And he said, The things which are impossible with men are possible with God.
28 Then Peter said, Lo, we have left all, and followed thee.
29 And he said unto them, Verily I say unto you, There is no man that hath left house, or parents, or brethren, or wife, or children, for the kingdom of God's sake,
30 Who shall not receive manifold more in this

present time, and in the world to come life
everlasting.

A Prediction of Death and Resurrection

31 Then he took unto him the twelve, and said unto
them, Behold, we go up to Jerusalem, and all things
that are written by the prophets concerning the Son
of man shall be accomplished.
32 For he shall be delivered unto the Gentiles, and
shall be mocked, and spitefully entreated, and
spitted on:
33 And they shall scourge him, and put him to death:
and the third day he shall rise again.
34 And they understood none of these things: and
this saying was hid from them, neither knew they
the things which were spoken.

18.31-34. The Lord's death and resurrection are graphically brought before them.
The life of the Lord involved the reality of sacrifice and it was imminent - all happening in Jerusalem (v31) as the Old Testament prophets had predicted. None of them were ready to hear these truths and so it passed them by (v34). Sometimes we pray for God to speak in reality and vividly - and when He does we cannot hear Him.

A Blind Man Near Jericho

35 And it came to pass, that as he was come nigh
unto Jericho, a certain blind man sat by the way
side begging:
36 And hearing the multitude pass by, he asked
what it meant.
37 And they told him, that Jesus of Nazareth passeth
by.
38 And he cried, saying, Jesus, thou son of David,
have mercy on me.
39 And they which went before rebuked him, that
he should hold his peace: but he cried so much the
more, Thou son of David, have mercy on me.
40 And Jesus stood, and commanded him to be
brought unto him: and when he was come near,
he asked him,
41 Saying, What wilt thou that I shall do unto thee?
And he said, Lord, that I may receive my sight.
42 And Jesus said unto him, Receive thy sight: thy
faith hath saved thee.
43 And immediately he received his sight, and
followed him, glorifying God: and all the people,
when they saw it, gave praise unto God.

18.35-43 Blind Bartimaeus gets his sight.
On the way to His death at Jerusalem the Lord's last stop is Jericho. The prayer of Bartimaeus is real. He cries to the Lord for mercy and does not stop even when encouraged to stop. The resistance just intensifies his prayer (v37-39). The Lord stands before him as King, Son of David (v38,40) and asks what he requires (v41). He asked for sight and got sight plus salvation (v42). This miracle symbolises the truth of the reality of our prayers and it brings glory to God (v43). It is not so much who is praying but to Whom we are praying that makes the difference for entering the kingdom.

Reflective Questions and Notes

A. What is the main point of the parable of the unjust judge? v1-9

B. What is the main point of the parable of the two men who go up to the temple to pray? v10-14

C. Read verses 25-27. Can anyone be saved? How?

D. How did Blind Bartimaeus get saved? v42, v39

Luke 19

The Lord Passes Through Jericho

1 And Jesus entered and passed through Jericho.

2 And, behold, there was a man named Zacchaeus, which was the chief among the publicans, and he was rich.

3 And he sought to see Jesus who he was; and could not for the press, because he was little of stature.

4 And he ran before, and climbed up into a sycomore tree to see him: for he was to pass that way.

5 And when Jesus came to the place, he looked up, and saw him, and said unto him, Zacchaeus, make haste, and come down; for to day I must abide at thy house.

6 And he made haste, and came down, and received him joyfully.

7 And when they saw it, they all murmured, saying, That he was gone to be guest with a man that is a sinner.

8 And Zacchaeus stood, and said unto the Lord: Behold, Lord, the half of my goods I give to the poor; and if I have taken any thing from any man by false accusation, I restore him fourfold.

9 And Jesus said unto him, This day is salvation come to this house, forsomuch as he also is a son of Abraham.

The Golden Text of Luke

10 For the Son of man is come to seek and to save that which was lost.

The Parable of the Ten Pounds

11 And as they heard these things, he added and spake a parable, because he was nigh to Jerusalem, and because they thought that the kingdom of God should immediately appear.

12 He said therefore, A certain nobleman went into a far country to receive for himself a kingdom, and to return.

13 And he called his ten servants, and delivered them ten pounds, and said unto them, Occupy till I come.

14 But his citizens hated him, and sent a message after him, saying, We will not have this man to reign over us.

The Lord entering Jerusalem - the Kingdom and faith

Luke 19.1-10 Zacchaeus' salvation.

As the Lord continues His journey to Jerusalem through Jericho, He meets another rich man (v2), a chief tax collector ('publican' v2), but this time (unlike the man in ch. 18) the man accepts the need to come as a child to Christ for salvation. Zacchaeus desired ('sought' v3) to see Christ and couldn't for the crowd ('press') and because he was small ('little of stature v3). Having climbed a tree (v4), the Saviour stood under it, named him personally and told him to come down. Salvation is a humbling matter and requires that we get down before Christ. Zacchaeus obeyed quickly ('haste' v6) and received Christ and knew the joy of salvation (v6-7). He put matters right for his previous sins – a changed man (v8-9). 'Fourfold' – means he gave back four times as much as he took. Zacchaeus had by exercising faith in Christ become a son of Abraham, the father of faith. He was now no longer lost.

19.11-27. Parable of the pounds This parable told in Jericho (v28) as a result of a belief that the kingdom was imminent (v11). The nobleman is a picture of Christ who would leave this world only to return to reign in His kingdom (v12). The servants are the disciples of Christ who in the days of His absence are all given responsibility as indicated by the pound (v13). The citizens could be Israel, but it certainly speaks of those who do not claim to be a disciple of Christ and do not want Him as king (v14). When He returns to reign in His kingdom the disciples will be rewarded for faithful service in his absence. The more faithful they are, the more they will be rewarded (v15-19) and extensive their roles will be in the kingdom. The disciple who has done nothing for his Lord in the days of His absence will lose out in reward and role in the kingdom, and be removed from the role of stewardship, suffering loss (v20-26). However, the enemies that rejected Him will be eternally judged (v27). The Lord is challenging His hearers about their conduct, in light of their belief about the imminence of the kingdom(v11). Are they ready for the return of the King? What role in the kingdom will they have? What are they doing now to prepare? There are three categories of hearers: (i) Those who had no faith in Christ and had rejected Him as King – they will be judged eternally; (ii) those who had come to Christ in faith and were seeking to serve Him by faith until He returns (man with ten pounds and five pounds) – they will be greatly rewarded; (iii) the disciple of Christ who was doing nothing for his Lord in the days of His absence and who will enter heaven on the basis of grace but lose out on reward and responsibility for not living by faith.

15 And it came to pass, that when he was returned, having received the kingdom, then he commanded these servants to be called unto him, to whom he had given the money, that he might know how much every man had gained by trading.

16 Then came the first, saying, Lord, thy pound hath gained ten pounds.

17 And he said unto him, Well, thou good servant: because thou hast been faithful in a very little, have thou authority over ten cities.

18 And the second came, saying, Lord, thy pound hath gained five pounds.

19 And he said likewise to him, Be thou also over five cities.

20 And another came, saying, Lord, behold, here is thy pound, which I have kept laid up in a napkin:

21 For I feared thee, because thou art an austere man: thou takest up that thou layedst not down, and reapest that thou didst not sow.

22 And he saith unto him, Out of thine own mouth will I judge thee, thou wicked servant. Thou knewest that I was an austere man, taking up that I laid not down, and reaping that I did not sow:

23 Wherefore then gavest not thou my money into the bank, that at my coming I might have required mine own with usury?

24 And he said unto them that stood by, Take from him the pound, and give it to him that hath ten pounds.

25 (And they said unto him, Lord, he hath ten pounds.)

26 For I say unto you, That unto every one which hath shall be given; and from him that hath not, even that he hath shall be taken away from him.

27 But those mine enemies, which would not that I should reign over them, bring hither, and slay them before me.

19.28-48. The King entering into Jerusalem. The Lord of Glory would ride on a donkey – what humility! The Lord of creation would ride in complete control

The Lord Enters Jerusalem on a Colt

28 And when he had thus spoken, he went before, ascending up to Jerusalem.

29 And it came to pass, when he was come nigh to Bethphage and Bethany, at the mount called the

mount of Olives, he sent two of his disciples,
30 Saying, Go ye into the village over against you;
in the which at your entering ye shall find a colt
tied, whereon yet never man sat: loose him, and
bring him hither.
31 And if any man ask you, Why do ye loose him?
thus shall ye say unto him, Because the Lord hath
need of him.
32 And they that were sent went their way, and
found even as he had said unto them.
33 And as they were loosing the colt, the owners
thereof said unto them, Why loose ye the colt?
34 And they said, The Lord hath need of him.
35 And they brought him to Jesus: and they cast
their garments upon the colt, and they set Jesus
thereon.
36 And as he went, they spread their clothes in
the way.
37 And when he was come nigh, even now at the
descent of the mount of Olives, the whole multitude
of the disciples began to rejoice and praise God
with a loud voice for all the mighty works that they
had seen;
38 Saying, Blessed be the King that cometh in the
name of the Lord: peace in heaven, and glory in
the highest.
39 And some of the Pharisees from among the
multitude said unto him, Master, rebuke thy
disciples.
40 And he answered and said unto them, I tell you
that, if these should hold their peace, the stones
would immediately cry out.

The Lord Weeps over Jerusalem

41 And when he was come near, he beheld the city,
and wept over it,
42 Saying, If thou hadst known, even thou, at least
in this thy day, the things which belong unto thy
peace! but now they are hid from thine eyes.
43 For the days shall come upon thee, that thine
enemies shall cast a trench about thee, and compass
thee round, and keep thee in on every side,
44 And shall lay thee even with the ground, and thy

on an unbroken donkey - what majesty!

19.31-34 When we are doing a work for the Lord there will always be interference. The answer is always the same 'The Lord has need of him/her'. They found that the events had all been pre-planned – 'even as He had said' – God is sovereign. It is wonderful when we know we are walking in His will.

19.35-40. The coronation of the King. Clothes were spread before Him, hearts are bursting with joy to God, memories flood the mind of His mighty acts, tongues lift up the words of the psalms (particularly Psalm 118.26) and extol the person of the Messiah.

19.39-40 Again, wherever the Person of Christ is exalted there will be opposition. The Pharisees demand that the Lord rebuke the disciples for their claims that He is the Messiah in worship. The Lord answers that if they did not sing the stones would! Even Creation knew the King, but Israel did not.

19.41-44 Israel's unwillingness to repent caused the Lord Jesus to cry – tears of real sorrow. The people that had been so favoured over the years and protected had now rejected their Messiah (v42). The result would be that judgment would fall upon the city which happened in AD70 and will happen in a much fuller way again at His return.

children within thee; and they shall not leave in thee
one stone upon another; because thou knewest not
the time of thy visitation.

19.45-48 The Lord Jesus claims the temple (God's House) to be His House ('My House') as One who is Divine and the true King of Kings.
They had turned the temple into a business and forgotten the sacredness of the place for prayer. These actions and His teaching and claims resulted in the Jewish leaders plotting to kill Him. Their evil plans were hindered by the large crowd of people that hung on His words.

The Lord Enters and Purifies the Temple

45 And he went into the temple, and began to cast
out them that sold therein, and them that bought;
46 Saying unto them, It is written, My house is
the house of prayer: but ye have made it a den of
thieves.
47 And he taught daily in the temple. But the chief
priests and the scribes and the chief of the people
sought to destroy him,
48 And could not find what they might do: for all
the people were very attentive to hear him.

Reflective Questions and Notes

A. Why has the Lord Jesus come? v10

B. Who are the three principal groups of people in the parable of the pounds? Which category are you in? v19-27

C. What is significant about the animal the Lord chose to ride upon to announce Himself as Messiah in Jerusalem? v30-38

D. Why is the Lord's claim and actions about the temple significant? v44-48

Luke 20

Chapter 20 The Lord's Power and Authority as King.

20.1-8. The Pharisees have a question about the origin of the authority and power of the Lord Jesus (v1-2). The Lord asks about John the Baptist's authority to baptise whether it was divine or human (v3-4)? This led the religious rulers into a political dilemma as everyone accepted John's authority was Divine, but they could not admit it – so they said they couldn't say (v5-7). Having established that the issue was not the evidence of their eyes but the will of their heart to believe, the Lord said He wouldn't explain then the basis of His authority, as they wouldn't believe (v8).

Who Gave Thee this Authority?

1 And it came to pass, that on one of those days, as he taught the people in the temple, and preached the gospel, the chief priests and the scribes came upon him with the elders,
2 And spake unto him, saying, Tell us, by what authority doest thou these things? or who is he that gave thee this authority?
3 And he answered and said unto them, I will also ask you one thing; and answer me:
4 The baptism of John, was it from heaven, or of men?
5 And they reasoned with themselves, saying, If we shall say, From heaven; he will say, Why then believed ye him not?
6 But and if we say, Of men; all the people will stone us: for they be persuaded that John was a prophet.
7 And they answered, that they could not tell whence it was.
8 And Jesus said unto them, Neither tell I you by what authority I do these things.

20.9-19. The parable of the vineyard.

The Lord proceeds to tell a parable without explaining it – but they still all understood it (v16, v19). The parable explains the authority of the Son of God and the hardness of the heart of Israel to His claims. The vineyard is Israel, the man who owns the vineyard is God, the husbandmen are those who have been entrusted to supervise the nation of Israel and bring fruit to God (v9). The servants are Old Testament prophets like Jeremiah and New Testament prophets like John the Baptist who when they came to Israel were beaten and killed (V10-12). The Beloved Son is the Lord Jesus (v13) who they crucified (v14-15). The Lord of the vineyard

I Will Send My Beloved Son

9 Then began he to speak to the people this parable; A certain man planted a vineyard, and let it forth to husbandmen, and went into a far country for a long time.
10 And at the season he sent a servant to the husbandmen, that they should give him of the fruit of the vineyard: but the husbandmen beat him, and sent him away empty.
11 And again he sent another servant: and they beat him also, and entreated him shamefully, and sent him away empty.
12 And again he sent a third: and they wounded him also, and cast him out.
13 Then said the lord of the vineyard, What shall I do? I will send my beloved son: it may be they will reverence him when they see him.
14 But when the husbandmen saw him, they reasoned among themselves, saying, This is the

heir: come, let us kill him, that the inheritance may
be ours.
15 So they cast him out of the vineyard, and killed
him. What therefore shall the lord of the vineyard
do unto them?
16 He shall come and destroy these husbandmen,
and shall give the vineyard to others. And when they
heard it, they said, God forbid.
17 And he beheld them, and said, What is this
then that is written, The stone which the builders
rejected, the same is become the head of the corner?
18 Whosoever shall fall upon that stone shall be
broken; but on whomsoever it shall fall, it will grind
him to powder.

Show Me a Penny

19 And the chief priests and the scribes the same
hour sought to lay hands on him; and they feared
the people: for they perceived that he had spoken
this parable against them.
20 And they watched him, and sent forth spies,
which should feign themselves just men, that they
might take hold of his words, that so they might
deliver him unto the power and authority of the
governor.
21 And they asked him, saying, Master, we know that
thou sayest and teachest rightly, neither acceptest
thou the person of any, but teachest the way of
God truly:
22 Is it lawful for us to give tribute unto Caesar,
or no?
23 But he perceived their craftiness, and said unto
them, Why tempt ye me?
24 Shew me a penny. Whose image and superscription
hath it? They answered and said, Caesar's.
25 And he said unto them, Render therefore unto
Caesar the things which be Caesar's, and unto God
the things which be God's.
26 And they could not take hold of his words before
the people: and they marvelled at his answer, and
held their peace.

The God of the Living

27 Then came to him certain of the Sadducees,

will destroy that nation and use people from other nations to bring fruit unto God and testify to His Salvation (v15-16). This last part of the story terrified the people (v16) and irritated the rulers (v19).

20.17-18 The Lord then quotes from Psalm 118.22 about the Messiah, using the analogy about the stone that was rejected that became the stone that all other stones in the building took its line from – the head corner stone. Falling upon Christ will break people's will in conviction of sin but grant salvation. The stone of judgment falling upon those who reject Him will utterly consume them.

20.20-26 A loaded political question about authority and power.
The Pharisees wanted the Christ to say something that would lead to Him coming under the power and authority of Rome. The question is carefully planted about the legality of Caesar's tax ('tribute'- v22). He knew they were pretending ('feign' v20) and deliberately testing Him by stealth ('craftiness'-v23). The Lord answers the question masterfully, asking for a penny and noting the image of Caesar and instructing to give to Caeser what belongs to Caeser and to God what belongs to God. This answer acknowledged that in civil affairs there was a delegated authority, but the ultimate authority was God.

20.27-40 A religious question and riddle about resurrection

power from the Sadducees. The question about the wife with seven husbands was carefully crafted to make it impossible to answer (v28-33). The scepticism of the Sadducees was a characteristic feature of their philosophy. Amongst other things, they did not believe in resurrection.

which deny that there is any resurrection; and they asked him,
28 Saying, Master, Moses wrote unto us, If any man's brother die, having a wife, and he die without children, that his brother should take his wife, and raise up seed unto his brother.
29 There were therefore seven brethren: and the first took a wife, and died without children.
30 And the second took her to wife, and he died childless.
31 And the third took her; and in like manner the seven also: and they left no children, and died.
32 Last of all the woman died also.
33 Therefore in the resurrection whose wife of them is she? for seven had her to wife.

20.34-36 The Lord showed them that the question begged their ignorance about the next life and the truth of Scripture. Marriage is for this life only. Sexual acts do not take place in heaven, but heaven's residents are like the angels, sons of God, reflecting the glory of the One who has saved them.

20.37-39 The Lord then proves that the resurrection is taught in Scripture from the book of Exodus chapter 3 from a 'present tense'. People do not cease to exist after they die. God is the God of Abraham now as He was centuries before. Abraham is alive and waiting for his resurrection body when the Lord returns to set up His kingdom. God will save the whole person – body, soul and spirit. This answer is publicly acknowledged by the scribe (perhaps a Pharisee) – v39.

20. 40-47. Their questions being finished (v40 – 'durst' means did') the Lord then asks a question about the power and authority of the Messiah from Psalm 110. 1. How can David call his Son, Lord? The question is not answered but all know that He is claiming

34 And Jesus answering said unto them, The children of this world marry, and are given in marriage:
35 But they which shall be accounted worthy to obtain that world, and the resurrection from the dead, neither marry, nor are given in marriage:
36 Neither can they die any more: for they are equal unto the angels; and are the children of God, being the children of the resurrection.
37 Now that the dead are raised, even Moses shewed at the bush, when he calleth the Lord the God of Abraham, and the God of Isaac, and the God of Jacob.
38 For he is not a God of the dead, but of the living: for all live unto him.
39 Then certain of the scribes answering said, Master, thou hast well said.
40 And after that they durst not ask him any question at all.

The Question about the Son of David

41 And he said unto them, How say they that Christ is David's son?
42 And David himself saith in the book of Psalms, The Lord said unto my Lord, Sit thou on my right hand,
43 Till I make thine enemies thy footstool.
44 David therefore calleth him Lord, how is he then his son?

45 Then in the audience of all the people he said
unto his disciples,
46 Beware of the scribes, which desire to walk in
long robes, and love greetings in the markets, and
the highest seats in the synagogues, and the chief
rooms at feasts;
47 Which devour widows' houses, and for a shew
make long prayers: the same shall receive greater
damnation.

as Messiah to be the Lord God. He then warns that the so-called authority and piety (v47) of these religious men can be seen in their actions longing for place, privilege and power (v46) at the direct expense of the poor (v47). Their religious hypocrisy will be judged even more severely (v47- 'greater damnation') for their greater responsibility.

Reflective Questions and Notes

A. Why did the Lord not answer their question? v2-8

B. How does the parable in verses 9-19 answer the question of verse 2?

C. What was their motive for asking the question of v22? See v20

D. What was the claim Christ was making in His question to the religious leaders in verses 40-44?

Luke 21

The Widow's Two Mites

1 And he looked up, and saw the rich men casting their gifts into the treasury.
2 And he saw also a certain poor widow casting in thither two mites.
3 And he said, Of a truth I say unto you, that this poor widow hath cast in more than they all:
4 For all these have of their abundance cast in unto the offerings of God: but she of her penury hath cast in all the living that she had.

When Shall These Things Be?

5 And as some spake of the temple, how it was adorned with goodly stones and gifts, he said,
6 As for these things which ye behold, the days will come, in the which there shall not be left one stone upon another, that shall not be thrown down.
7 And they asked him, saying, Master, but when shall these things be? and what sign will there be when these things shall come to pass?
8 And he said, Take heed that ye be not deceived: for many shall come in my name, saying, I am Christ; and the time draweth near: go ye not therefore after them.
9 But when ye shall hear of wars and commotions, be not terrified: for these things must first come to pass; but the end is not by and by.
10 Then said he unto them, Nation shall rise against nation, and kingdom against kingdom:
11 And great earthquakes shall be in divers places, and famines, and pestilences; and fearful sights and great signs shall there be from heaven.
12 But before all these, they shall lay their hands on you, and persecute you, delivering you up to the synagogues, and into prisons, being brought before kings and rulers for my name's sake.
13 And it shall turn to you for a testimony.
14 Settle it therefore in your hearts, not to meditate before what ye shall answer:
15 For I will give you a mouth and wisdom, which all your adversaries shall not be able to gainsay nor resist.

Chapter 21 The Lord's last few days - His teaching about the temple

21.1-4 Having discussed how judgment will be more severe towards religious men who rob poor widows, the Lord turns to look at the treasury (collection box) at the temple. It was there that rich people flamboyantly gave money to the temple (v1) and then He saw a poor widow who donated two mites (the coin with the lowest value). The Lord said she had given more than all the rich men for they gave out of their riches, but she gave out of her poverty (v2- 'penury'), everything she had. God's rewards, as well as his retribution, are based on responsibility (see 20. 47).

21.5-38 The temple and its destruction at the coming of the Son of Man.

21.5-7 The fact that some were so impressed with the stones, wealth and majesty of the temple led Him to tell them how it was all going to be destroyed. This literally happened in AD 70 but much of what He said also relates to the point when He will return to set up His kingdom in the future (v7, v 27).

21.8-19 The signs prior to the coming of the Son of man will be marked by religious confusion (v8); military aggression (v9 -10); international pandemics (v11); raging anti-Semitism and persecution for believers (v12). All of this will bring opportunity to believers to testify for Christ and the simple believer will be given words to say (v12-15). Another feature of this period will be the breakdown of families and the rise of individualism(v16) with the unnatural situation of families betraying one another.

21.17-19 There is an encouragement to the believer, however, that they will be preserved despite the hatred. Verse 19 can read as follows: 'By your endurance you will gain your lives'.

21.20-26 The other sign that will happen prior to the coming of the Lord Jesus is the complete destruction of Jerusalem including the temple. Armies from various countries will surround Israel (v20); people will flee for safety which will be dreadful for those women that are pregnant and the vulnerable (v21-23). Israel will be defeated, and many will be taken hostage by foreign powers until the Lord comes (v24). During this time strange happenings will take place in the stellar heavens and in the oceans (v25) causing huge distress (v26).

21.27-33. The Lord comes back. This is the point when the Lord Jesus will return with power and great glory (v27). This will cause all the faithful to Christ to rejoice (v28) for the day of their deliverance ('redemption') has come. Just as fig trees produce leaves indicating fruit will come at a specific time, just as surely all these signs will indicate that the Messiah is coming back again (v29-31). Israel ('this generation') will not be eliminated, all these things will happen (v32). The

16 And ye shall be betrayed both by parents, and brethren, and kinsfolks, and friends; and some of you shall they cause to be put to death.
17 And ye shall be hated of all men for my name's sake.
18 But there shall not an hair of your head perish.
19 In your patience possess ye your souls.
20 And when ye shall see Jerusalem compassed with armies, then know that the desolation thereof is nigh.
21 Then let them which are in Judaea flee to the mountains; and let them which are in the midst of it depart out; and let not them that are in the countries enter thereinto.
22 For these be the days of vengeance, that all things which are written may be fulfilled.
23 But woe unto them that are with child, and to them that give suck, in those days! for there shall be great distress in the land, and wrath upon this people.
24 And they shall fall by the edge of the sword, and shall be led away captive into all nations: and Jerusalem shall be trodden down of the Gentiles, until the times of the Gentiles be fulfilled.
25 And there shall be signs in the sun, and in the moon, and in the stars; and upon the earth distress of nations, with perplexity; the sea and the waves roaring;
26 Men's hearts failing them for fear, and for looking after those things which are coming on the earth: for the powers of heaven shall be shaken.
27 And then shall they see the Son of man coming in a cloud with power and great glory.
28 And when these things begin to come to pass, then look up, and lift up your heads; for your redemption draweth nigh.
29 And he spake to them a parable; Behold the fig tree, and all the trees;
30 When they now shoot forth, ye see and know of your own selves that summer is now nigh at hand.
31 So likewise ye, when ye see these things come to pass, know ye that the kingdom of God is nigh at hand.

32 Verily I say unto you, This generation shall not
pass away, till all be fulfilled.
33 Heaven and earth shall pass away: but my words
shall not pass away.
34 And take heed to yourselves, lest at any time
your hearts be overcharged with surfeiting, and
drunkenness, and cares of this life, and so that day
come upon you unawares.
35 For as a snare shall it come on all them that dwell
on the face of the whole earth.
36 Watch ye therefore, and pray always, that ye may
be accounted worthy to escape all these things
that shall come to pass, and to stand before the
Son of man.

A Summary of Days Spent in Jerusalem

37 And in the day time he was teaching in the
temple; and at night he went out, and abode in the
mount that is called the mount of Olives.
38 And all the people came early in the morning to
him in the temple, for to hear him.

universe could pass away, but the Word of Christ can never pass away (v33).

21.34-38 A warning by the Lord Jesus in the light of these things. He warns that disciples should not be consumed with this world, its pleasures and its cares – it is passing away. (v34 'surfeiting' – means 'carousing'- open drunkenness). He requests that belivers are sober and sincere and that they pray for grace to stand for Christ when the persecution arises (v35-36).

All these truths were taught to the people in the temple precincts before He went out to pray at the Mount of Olives (v37-38).

Reflective Questions and Notes

A. Why had the widow women given more than anyone else? v1-7

B. What are the signs that will precede the coming again of the Lord Jesus to the earth to set up His kingdom? v8-19

C. When will they know that He is about to come very soon? v20-33

D. How should these amazing truths affect believers in the Lord Jesus? v34-38

Luke 22

Judas Conspires with the High Priests

1 Now the feast of unleavened bread drew nigh,
which is called the Passover.
2 And the chief priests and scribes sought how they
might kill him; for they feared the people.
3 Then entered Satan into Judas surnamed Iscariot,
being of the number of the twelve.
4 And he went his way, and communed with the
chief priests and captains, how he might betray
him unto them.
5 And they were glad, and covenanted to give him
money.
6 And he promised, and sought opportunity
to betray him unto them in the absence of the
multitude.

The Large Upper Room

7 Then came the day of unleavened bread, when
the passover must be killed.
8 And he sent Peter and John, saying, Go and
prepare us the passover, that we may eat.
9 And they said unto him, Where wilt thou that we
prepare?
10 And he said unto them, Behold, when ye are
entered into the city, there shall a man meet you,
bearing a pitcher of water; follow him into the house
where he entereth in.
11 And ye shall say unto the goodman of the
house, The Master saith unto thee, Where is the
guestchamber, where I shall eat the passover with
my disciples?
12 And he shall shew you a large upper room
furnished: there make ready.
13 And they went, and found as he had said unto
them: and they made ready the passover.

The Lord Keeps the Passover

14 And when the hour was come, he sat down, and
the twelve apostles with him.
15 And he said unto them, With desire I have desired
to eat this passover with you before I suffer:
16 For I say unto you, I will not any more eat thereof,
until it be fulfilled in the kingdom of God.

Chapter 22 The Lord's last night before the Cross.

22.1-38 The Lord with His own at the supper table.
The annual gathering for Passover, a commemoration of Israel coming out of Egypt (Exodus 12), was taking place and thousands would arrive in Jerusalem for this holy week (v1).
22.2-6 Opposition was mounting against the Lord Jesus externally (v2) and internally (v3-4). Judas Iscariot shows himself to be a fraud, motivated by money (v5) not spirituality (v6).

22.7-13 Preparation of the Passover meal.
Peter and John are both entrusted with the task of locating the guest room ('guestchamber' v11) that the Lord had already secured and preparing the meal. They were to follow an unnamed man who carried a large jar ('pitcher' v10) of water. It must have been incredible when they went and saw the man and everything happening 'as He had said' (v13). To move in the will of God is exciting. The water the man carried would have been needed for the Lord to wash the disciples' feet (John 13).

22.14-18 The Passover meal.
The 'hour' (v14) of the Passover day was at 6.00 pm at the commence of Nisan 14, their first month of the year around March/April. This 'hour' has long been in the calendar of God as the day the Saviour would die. He desired to eat the Passover and then

suffer for the sins of the world (v15). After eating the Passover meal, the Lord would no longer eat (v16) or drink (v18) anything until His suffering, which had long been predicted in Scripture, was fulfilled.

22.19-20 The Breaking of Bread. The Lord then established that disciples should remember Him by partaking of bread and wine as a remembrance of His body and blood, His life and death on their behalf. This began to take place after His resurrection in local assemblies of Christians on the first day of the week (Acts 20.7).

22.21-38 Betrayal, boasting and denial of the disciples.

The death and betrayal of the Lord Jesus had been prophesied in Scripture hundreds of years before ('as it was determined') but the man that did it (Judas Iscariot) would still be held eternally responsible for his actions (v22-23). This solemn statement makes the disciples vow their allegiance to Christ leading to pride regarding who was the greatest and most special to Christ(v24). The Lord reminds them that this type of hierarchical behaviour is what marks the rulers of this world (v25) but not His kingdom. Those who are greatest are those who are lowest, leaders serve others (v27). The disciples had been with Him through trial and all will be blessed in the future kingdom and have the privilege of eating and drinking at His table and being permitted to sit in judgment over Israel in a future day. Therefore, none of them were to start thinking that they were better than anyone else (v28-30). The Lord then turns to Peter calling him by his old name 'Simon' twice, and warns him of a

17 And he took the cup, and gave thanks, and said,
Take this, and divide it among yourselves:
18 For I say unto you, I will not drink of the fruit of
the vine, until the kingdom of God shall come.

The Institution of the Lord's Supper

19 And he took bread, and gave thanks, and brake it,
and gave unto them, saying, This is my body which
is given for you: this do in remembrance of me.
20 Likewise also the cup after supper, saying, This
cup is the new testament in my blood, which is
shed for you.

Who Shall be Accounted the Greatest?

21 But, behold, the hand of him that betrayeth me
is with me on the table.
22 And truly the Son of man goeth, as it was
determined: but woe unto that man by whom he
is betrayed!
23 And they began to enquire among themselves,
which of them it was that should do this thing.
24 And there was also a strife among them, which
of them should be accounted the greatest.
25 And he said unto them, The kings of the Gentiles
exercise lordship over them; and they that exercise
authority upon them are called benefactors.
26 But ye shall not be so: but he that is greatest
among you, let him be as the younger; and he that
is chief, as he that doth serve.
27 For whether is greater, he that sitteth at meat, or
he that serveth? is not he that sitteth at meat? but
I am among you as he that serveth.
28 Ye are they which have continued with me in my
temptations.
29 And I appoint unto you a kingdom, as my Father
hath appointed unto me;
30 That ye may eat and drink at my table in my
kingdom, and sit on thrones judging the twelve
tribes of Israel.

The Lord foretells Peter's Denial

31 And the Lord said, Simon, Simon, behold, Satan
hath desired to have you, that he may sift you as
wheat:
32 But I have prayed for thee, that thy faith fail

not: and when thou art converted, strengthen thy
brethren.
33 And he said unto him, Lord, I am ready to go with
thee, both into prison, and to death.
34 And he said, I tell thee, Peter, the cock shall not
crow this day, before that thou shalt thrice deny
that thou knowest me.

Beloved, Here are Two Swords

35 And he said unto them, When I sent you without
purse, and scrip, and shoes, lacked ye any thing?
And they said, Nothing.
36 Then said he unto them, But now, he that hath a
purse, let him take it, and likewise his scrip: and he that
hath no sword, let him sell his garment, and buy one.
37 For I say unto you, that this that is written must
yet be accomplished in me, And he was reckoned
among the transgressors: for the things concerning
me have an end.
38 And they said, Lord, behold, here are two swords.
And he said unto them, It is enough.

The Agony in the Garden

39 And he came out, and went, as he was wont, to
the mount of Olives; and his disciples also followed
him.
40 And when he was at the place, he said unto them,
Pray that ye enter not into temptation.
41 And he was withdrawn from them about a stone's
cast, and kneeled down, and prayed,
42 Saying, Father, if thou be willing, remove this
cup from me: nevertheless not my will, but thine,
be done.
43 And there appeared an angel unto him from
heaven, strengthening him.
44 And being in an agony he prayed more earnestly:
and his sweat was as it were great drops of blood
falling down to the ground.
45 And when he rose up from prayer, and was come
to his disciples, he found them sleeping for sorrow,
46 And said unto them, Why sleep ye? rise and pray,
lest ye enter into temptation.

This is Your Hour

47 And while he yet spake, behold a multitude, and

satanic attack (v31). Peter says he is ready to die for the Lord (v33). The Lord tells him that he will deny Him three times that night, before the rooster crows in the morning! (v34). The Lord then equips them for the long night ahead when He would die for sin. He asked them to take some provisions - take your money bag, and your knapsack ('scrip' – v35). Finally, He asked them to get a sword (v37-38), He would soon teach them the lesson of the undrawn sword (v49-51).

22.39-53 The Garden of Gethsemane.

They came as was His custom ('wont' v39) to the slopes of Olivet to pray. Other Gospels call it Gethsemane. It is here that He went ahead of the disciples a stone's throw further and prays alone. His prayer which He uttered three times is most significant. He anticipated the awfulness of Calvary and the fact that He was going to be held accountable for the sin of the world and establish a righteous basis for the forgiveness of sins. His holy soul recoils from sin ('remove this cup from me') and yet in complete obedience He utters three times 'not my will but thine be done'. The intensity of this prayer causes the sweat to be so viscous as to appear like blood (v44). He rises to find the disciples sleeping (v45-46) and Judas coming with soldiers to betray Him with a deceitful kiss (v47-48). Some of the disciples think that the answer is to draw the sword, they still do not know that this the will of God for His Son. The undrawn sword is His way. One of the disciples (Peter – John 18.10) slashes a man's ear off and the Lord's last act is one of grace as He stoops to pick up the ear and put it back on the man's head (v51). The Lord rebukes the religious rulers for behaving like thieves by their underhand manner of taking Him at night with swords and clubs when He was each day in the temple teaching them. However, He adds, solemnly,'This is your hour'. The hour of wickedness, when the power of darkness can be no darker (v53), when the Saviour of the world will be 'numbered with the transgressors' and His life will come to 'an end' (v37).

22.54-65 House of the High Priest. They arrested the Lord Jesus and took him to Annas and Caiaphas the High Priest. Peter (and John- John 18.15) come into the forecourt of the High Priest's house and sat by a fire while the Lord was being interrogated inside (v54-55). A servant girl accuses Peter of belonging to Christ which he denies three times (v56-60), On the last time the rooster crows for the morning, as the Lord had said (v34, v60-61). At this exact point the Lord looks directly at Peter and Peter leaves, crying bitter tears of repentance and sorrow (v61-62). The Lord experienced being verbally and physically abused (v63- 'smote' – struck him with fists and clubs) and psychological abuse involving a blindfold and blasphemous attacks (v64-65).

he that was called Judas, one of the twelve, went
before them, and drew near unto Jesus to kiss him.
48 But Jesus said unto him, Judas, betrayest thou
the Son of man with a kiss?
49 When they which were about him saw what
would follow, they said unto him, Lord, shall we
smite with the sword?
50 And one of them smote the servant of the high
priest, and cut off his right ear.
51 And Jesus answered and said, Suffer ye thus far.
And he touched his ear, and healed him.
52 Then Jesus said unto the chief priests, and
captains of the temple, and the elders, which were
come to him, Be ye come out, as against a thief, with
swords and staves?
53 When I was daily with you in the temple, ye
stretched forth no hands against me: but this is your
hour, and the power of darkness.

The High Priest's Palace and Peter's Denial

54 Then took they him, and led him, and brought
him into the high priest's house. And Peter followed
afar off.
55 And when they had kindled a fire in the midst
of the hall, and were set down together, Peter sat
down among them.
56 But a certain maid beheld him as he sat by the
fire, and earnestly looked upon him, and said, This
man was also with him.
57 And he denied him, saying, Woman, I know him
not.
58 And after a little while another saw him, and said,
Thou art also of them. And Peter said, Man, I am not.
59 And about the space of one hour after another
confidently affirmed, saying, Of a truth this fellow
also was with him: for he is a Galilaean.
60 And Peter said, Man, I know not what thou sayest.
And immediately, while he yet spake, the cock crew.
61 And the Lord turned, and looked upon Peter.
And Peter remembered the word of the Lord, how
he had said unto him, Before the cock crow, thou
shalt deny me thrice.
62 And Peter went out, and wept bitterly.

63 And the men that held Jesus mocked him, and smote him.
64 And when they had blindfolded him, they struck him on the face, and asked him, saying, Prophesy, who is it that smote thee?
65 And many other things blasphemously spake they against him.

The Lord Jesus before the Council

66 And as soon as it was day, the elders of the people and the chief priests and the scribes came together, and led him into their council, saying,
67 Art thou the Christ? tell us. And he said unto them, If I tell you, ye will not believe:
68 And if I also ask you, ye will not answer me, nor let me go.
69 Hereafter shall the Son of man sit on the right hand of the power of God.
70 Then said they all, Art thou then the Son of God? And he said unto them, Ye say that I am.
71 And they said, What need we any further witness? for we ourselves have heard of his own mouth.

22.66-71 The Sanhedrin

A formal Sanhedrin (Jewish counsel) is called early on the morning of the Passover (v66). Their key question was to ask the Lord if He was the Messiah (the Christ)? He told them that their motivation for asking the question was not genuine, if He affirmed it they would not believe Him, nor would they let Him go (v67-68). He then affirmed that the Messiah would shortly be sitting in heaven at the right hand of God (v69). They asked if He was the Son of God and He confirmed it (v70- 'Ye say that I am' is a Hebrew idiom for 'You have said it – Yes'). The reply led them to stop the tribunal hearing (without asking for any witnesses or any more questions about character or evidence to validate His statements) as they had reached their conclusion – He was guilty of claiming to be the eternal Son of the eternal God.

Reflective Questions and Notes

A. What did the Lord command His disciples to do after He had died? v19-20

B. How did the Lord expect His disciples to behave after He had left them for heaven? v24-30

C. What was the Lord's last miracle in Luke's gospel? Any lessons for us? v49-51

D. What was the claim of Christ that caused the Sanhedrin to take Him to Pilate to be crucified? v67-71

____

____

____

____

____

Luke 23

The Lord Jesus before Pilate

1 And the whole multitude of them arose, and led him unto Pilate.

2 And they began to accuse him, saying, We found this fellow perverting the nation, and forbidding to give tribute to Caesar, saying that he himself is Christ a King.

3 And Pilate asked him, saying, Art thou the King of the Jews? And he answered him and said, Thou sayest it.

4 Then said Pilate to the chief priests and to the people, I find no fault in this man.

5 And they were the more fierce, saying, He stirreth up the people, teaching throughout all Jewry, beginning from Galilee to this place.

The Lord before Herod

6 When Pilate heard of Galilee, he asked whether the man were a Galilaean.

7 And as soon as he knew that he belonged unto Herod's jurisdiction, he sent him to Herod, who himself also was at Jerusalem at that time.

8 And when Herod saw Jesus, he was exceeding glad: for he was desirous to see him of a long season, because he had heard many things of him; and he hoped to have seen some miracle done by him.

9 Then he questioned with him in many words; but he answered him nothing.

10 And the chief priests and scribes stood and vehemently accused him.

11 And Herod with his men of war set him at nought, and mocked him, and arrayed him in a gorgeous robe, and sent him again to Pilate.

12 And the same day Pilate and Herod were made friends together: for before they were at enmity between themselves.

Christ or Barabbas?

13 And Pilate, when he had called together the chief priests and the rulers and the people,

14 Said unto them, Ye have brought this man unto me, as one that perverteth the people: and, behold, I, having examined him before you, have found no

Chapter 23 The Crucifixion of Christ.

23.1-7 Interview with Pilate and Christ. The Sanhedrin breaks up, and the crowd lead Christ to the Roman Governor Pontius Pilate (v1). They accuse Him (v2) of telling others to pay tax to the Romans (which is a lie – see 20. 22-26 and could not be verified) and of being the Christ (which is true). Pilate enquires about Him being the Messiah, the King which Christ confirms (v3). Pilate remarkably states he cannot find a fault in Christ (v4). This stirs the Jews into a frenzy saying the Lord is inciting people all over Israel to rebel against Rome (v5-which is a lie). Instead of doing what would be just and throw this matter out of court, Pilate sees an opportunity to delegate it and let someone else deal with the problem. Realising that the Lord Jesus was born in Galilee he sends Him to Herod who was currently in Jerusalem and had responsibility for that part of the country (v6-7).

23.8-11 The Lord before Herod. Herod had desired to see Christ many times (Luke 9. 9). He had an eye for the spectacular but not the spiritual (v8). The Lord stood in silence before him – His silence spoke to Herod about his sin in killing John the Baptist (Mark 6. 27). This led Herod to abuse and ridicule the person of Christ sending Him back to Pilate in a robe normally given to kings in mockery (v10-11). This act of mockery against Christ brought a friendship between arch rivals (v12).

23.13-19 Pilate's compromise. Pilate thought that although he could not give justice he could provide a political solution. He publicly proclaimed the Lord's innocence. Herod also had cleared Christ of all charges (v14-15). Pilate, however, still ordered the Saviour to be whipped (v16) in order to appease the angry crowd. He also said he would keep the custom of releasing a prisoner at the Passover time and instead of releasing a well-known murderer Barabbas he intended to release the Lord Jesus. He did not predict that his compromise would be rejected and that the crowd would want him to release the murderer instead (v17-19).

23.20-25 Pilate's fatal decision. Pilate is anxious for the Christ to be released and speaks to the crowd for a second time only to be drowned out with the screams of 'Crucify him' (v20-21). Pilate attempts a third time to explain to the crowd that the Lord Jesus was innocent having done no evil. He states that he will whip the Saviour again before release to please them, but they desired His death on a cross. Pilate eventually gives in to the mob's request and sentences the Saviour to die and releases the murderer Barabbas (v22-25).

23.26-32 The journey to the Cross. Racist behaviour is employed as they commandeer a black man ('Cyrenian') to carry the cross after the Lord Jesus (v26). The Lord speaks gently but solemnly to the weeping women who followed Him about coming judgment on the nation (v29-31). Alongside the sinless Lord Jesus are two robbers who will also be crucified. This fulfilled the prophesy of 22.37 – 'He was numbered amongst the transgressors'.

fault in this man touching those things whereof ye
accuse him:
15 No, nor yet Herod: for I sent you to him; and, lo,
nothing worthy of death is done unto him.
16 I will therefore chastise him, and release him.
17 (For of necessity he must release one unto them
at the feast.)
18 And they cried out all at once, saying, Away with
this man, and release unto us Barabbas:
19 (Who for a certain sedition made in the city, and
for murder, was cast into prison.)
20 Pilate therefore, willing to release Jesus, spake
again to them.
21 But they cried, saying, Crucify him, crucify him.
22 And he said unto them the third time, Why, what
evil hath he done? I have found no cause of death
in him: I will therefore chastise him, and let him go.
23 And they were instant with loud voices, requiring
that he might be crucified. And the voices of them
and of the chief priests prevailed.
24 And Pilate gave sentence that it should be as
they required.
25 And he released unto them him that for sedition
and murder was cast into prison, whom they had
desired; but he delivered Jesus to their will.

The Place Called Calvary

26 And as they led him away, they laid hold upon
one Simon, a Cyrenian, coming out of the country,
and on him they laid the cross, that he might bear
it after Jesus.
27 And there followed him a great company of
people, and of women, which also bewailed and
lamented him.
28 But Jesus turning unto them said, Daughters
of Jerusalem, weep not for me, but weep for
yourselves, and for your children.
29 For, behold, the days are coming, in the which
they shall say, Blessed are the barren, and the
wombs that never bare, and the paps which never
gave suck.
30 Then shall they begin to say to the mountains,
Fall on us; and to the hills, Cover us.

31 For if they do these things in a green tree, what
shall be done in the dry?
32 And there were also two other, malefactors, led
with him to be put to death.
33 And when they were come to the place, which
is called Calvary, there they crucified him, and the
malefactors, one on the right hand, and the other
on the left.
34 Then said Jesus, Father, forgive them; for they
know not what they do. And they parted his raiment,
and cast lots.
35 And the people stood beholding. And the rulers
also with them derided him, saying, He saved others;
let him save himself, if he be Christ, the chosen of God.
36 And the soldiers also mocked him, coming to
him, and offering him vinegar,
37 And saying, If thou be the king of the Jews, save
thyself.
38 And a superscription also was written over him
in letters of Greek, and Latin, and Hebrew, This Is
The King Of The Jews.

Two Malefactors

39 And one of the malefactors which were hanged
railed on him, saying, If thou be Christ, save thyself
and us.
40 But the other answering rebuked him, saying,
Dost not thou fear God, seeing thou art in the same
condemnation?
41 And we indeed justly; for we receive the due
reward of our deeds: but this man hath done
nothing amiss.
42 And he said unto Jesus, Lord, remember me when
thou comest into thy kingdom.
43 And Jesus said unto him, Verily I say unto thee,
Today shalt thou be with me in paradise.

Noonday Darkness

44 And it was about the sixth hour, and there was
a darkness over all the earth until the ninth hour.
45 And the sun was darkened, and the veil of the
temple was rent in the midst.

The Lord Dismisses His Spirit

46 And when Jesus had cried with a loud voice, he

22.33-49 The crucifixion of Christ. The first cry from Christ on the cross is one of forgiveness as they gambled ('cast lots') for His clothes (v34) and mocked the person of Christ (v35-37). They all suggest that He cannot save (v35, v37, v39) whereas in fact through His death He would be able to save all from their sins (1 Cor. 15. 3-4). A board with some writing (v38 -'superscription') above His head was written in three languages that He was the King. One of the robbers who was also on a cross spoke to his fellow robber directly. He shows that they were getting what they deserved (v40-41 'due reward of our deeds' – our just deserts!) but not Christ. He was sinless and perfect ('nothing amiss' v41). He turns to the Lord and called Him 'Lord' (v42). He took the place of being a servant subject to Christ. 'Remember me' – He took the place of being a sinner who needed salvation. 'Thy kingdom' – He knew the Lord Jesus was a Sovereign who had a kingdom and he wanted to be part of it (v42). The Saviour replied, 'Verily' (which means 'Truly') you 'will be with me today in Paradise (another word for heaven).' What love! What power! What assurance!

In verse 44-46 the Saviour enters into the darkness of Calvary. It is here that 'His soul is made an offering for sin' (Isaiah 53. 10). It is here that God the Father judged His son for the whole world so that access to God would be possible, this is seen symbolically in the tearing (v45'-'rent') in two of the veil in the temple that covered the way into the Holiest of all (v45). He with a loud voice

dismissed
His spirit (v46). He, unlike all others, chose to die.

23.47-56 The events immediately after the death of Christ are significant. A Roman Centurion finds salvation (v47). Joseph a Jewish man seeks permission to bury Christ in his own tomb and does so with real tenderness (v50-53). Some women who had witnessed His death (v49) took note of His grave and returned to their homes to make embalming ointments for the body (v54-56), resting on the special sabbath on the first day of unleavened bread and on the Saturday (23. 54, 56).

said, Father, into thy hands I commend my spirit: and having said thus, he gave up the ghost.

Witnesses

47 Now when the centurion saw what was done, he glorified God, saying, Certainly this was a righteous man.

48 And all the people that came together to that sight, beholding the things which were done, smote their breasts, and returned.

49 And all his acquaintance, and the women that followed him from Galilee, stood afar off, beholding these things.

The Burial of the Lord Jesus

50 And, behold, there was a man named Joseph, a counsellor; and he was a good man, and a just:

51 (The same had not consented to the counsel and deed of them;) he was of Arimathaea, a city of the Jews: who also himself waited for the kingdom of God.

52 This man went unto Pilate, and begged the body of Jesus.

53 And he took it down, and wrapped it in linen, and laid it in a sepulchre that was hewn in stone, wherein never man before was laid.

54 And that day was the preparation, and the sabbath drew on.

55 And the women also, which came with him from Galilee, followed after, and beheld the sepulchre, and how his body was laid.

56 And they returned, and prepared spices and ointments; and rested the sabbath day according to the commandment.

Reflective Questions and Notes

A. What did Pilate know about Christ? (v4, 14, 22)

B. What did one of the dying robbers know about Christ? (v40-43)

C. What happened in the darkness of Calvary? Why is the tearing of the veil in the temple significant? (v44-46)

D. What do a Roman centurion and a devout Jew have in common? (v47, 50-51)

Luke 24

Chapter 24 The Resurrection and Ascension of Christ.
4.1 -11 An early Sunday morning visit to the tomb by women. Three women (v10) waited till the third day (Sunday) before they came to the tomb with their spices and ointments (v1). To their consternation, the body of Christ was not there, and the large stone had been rolled away (v2-3). Two angels appeared like men enquiring why they were seeking a dead Christ when He had told them He would be crucified and rise again on the third day on many occasions (v4-7). At this point they remember the words of Christ and run to tell the eleven disciples. However, their testimony is, sadly, not believed (v8-11). The word of virtuous women like Joanna (Luke 8.3) wife of a steward to Herod, Mary the mother of James and Mary Magdalene (Luke 8.2) is treated with disbelief, like story telling ('idle tales').

He is Not Here, But is Risen

1 Now upon the first day of the week, very early in the morning, they came unto the sepulchre, bringing the spices which they had prepared, and certain others with them.

2 And they found the stone rolled away from the sepulchre.

3 And they entered in, and found not the body of the Lord Jesus.

4 And it came to pass, as they were much perplexed thereabout, behold, two men stood by them in shining garments:

5 And as they were afraid, and bowed down their faces to the earth, they said unto them, Why seek ye the living among the dead?

6 He is not here, but is risen: remember how he spake unto you when he was yet in Galilee,

7 Saying, The Son of man must be delivered into the hands of sinful men, and be crucified, and the third day rise again.

8 And they remembered his words,

9 And returned from the sepulchre, and told all these things unto the eleven, and to all the rest.

10 It was Mary Magdalene and Joanna, and Mary the mother of James, and other women that were with them, which told these things unto the apostles.

11 And their words seemed to them as idle tales, and they believed them not.

24.12 Peter responds to the women's story by running to the empty tomb ('sepulchre') and notes the ordered arrangement of the burial clothes and leaves thinking carefully on this evidence.

12 Then arose Peter, and ran unto the sepulchre; and stooping down, he beheld the linen clothes laid by themselves, and departed, wondering in himself at that which was come to pass.

24.13-32. Two on the road to Emmaus.
Two upset disciples make their way back 8 miles ('60 furlongs' v13) to their home in Emmaus discussing animatedly the things that have recently taken place, and hardly noticing a stranger (the Lord Jesus Christ) joining

The Road to Emmaus

13 And, behold, two of them went that same day to a village called Emmaus, which was from Jerusalem about threescore furlongs.

14 And they talked together of all these things which had happened.

15 And it came to pass, that, while they communed together and reasoned, Jesus himself drew near, and went with them.

16 But their eyes were holden that they should not
know him.
17 And he said unto them, What manner of
communications are these that ye have one to
another, as ye walk, and are sad?
18 And the one of them, whose name was Cleopas,
answering said unto him, Art thou only a stranger
in Jerusalem, and hast not known the things which
are come to pass there in these days?
19 And he said unto them, What things? And they
said unto him, Concerning Jesus of Nazareth, which
was a prophet mighty in deed and word before God
and all the people:
20 And how the chief priests and our rulers delivered
him to be condemned to death, and have crucified
him.
21 But we trusted that it had been he which should
have redeemed Israel: and beside all this, to day is
the third day since these things were done.
22 Yea, and certain women also of our company
made us astonished, which were early at the
sepulchre;
23 And when they found not his body, they came,
saying, that they had also seen a vision of angels,
which said that he was alive.
24 And certain of them which were with us went to
the sepulchre, and found it even so as the women
had said: but him they saw not.
25 Then he said unto them, O fools, and slow of
heart to believe all that the prophets have spoken:
26 Ought not Christ to have suffered these things,
and to enter into his glory?
27 And beginning at Moses and all the prophets,
he expounded unto them in all the scriptures the
things concerning himself.
28 And they drew nigh unto the village, whither
they went: and he made as though he would have
gone further.
29 But they constrained him, saying, Abide with us:
for it is toward evening, and the day is far spent. And
he went in to tarry with them.
30 And it came to pass, as he sat at meat with them,

them on the walk. They certainly do not recognise Christ – grief blinds- and their eyes are 'holden -v16' i.e. 'bound' from seeing Who He is (v13-16). The Lord asks them what they are talking about and why they are so sad? (v17). One of them called Cleopas (v18- possibly they are a husband and wife, John 19. 25) begins to tell them the whole story of the life, and death of Christ (v18-20). They express their disappointment that the kingdom on earth was not established and seem to think that since this is the third day that a fatal lapse of time has taken place since His death for anything significant to happen now. They also tell of the women's testimony of an empty tomb (which they accept as fact) and of His resurrection which they clearly find hard to believe (v21-24).

24.25-27 The Lord speaks.
The Lord calls them unwise ('fool') and slow to believe the clear teaching of Holy Scripture. He showed them from the beginning of their Bible (the books of Moses) to the end (the Prophets) that it predicts that the Messiah (Christ) must suffer and die and then be resurrected before ascending back to the glory of heaven.

24.28-32 At Supper in Emmaus.
When they arrive at Emmaus the Lord does not assume He can come to their home but waits for an invitation (v28-29 'Abide' – 'stay with us'). At the

meal time as He took bread and gave thanks for the food then their eyes were opened to see Him, and they recognised that He was the resurrected Christ. At the point of revelation, the Lord Jesus leaves them suddenly. (v30-31). Elated, they run back all the way to Jerusalem to tell the others, as they go they speak about their hearts burning in love as He had shown them so tenderly from the Scriptures what would happen to the Messiah (v32-33).

24.34-49 The Upper Room with Christ and His Disciples.

As they arrive in Jerusalem they learn from the other disciples that the Lord Jesus has risen and also appeared directly to Simon Peter (v34). The two disciples from Emmaus tell their story of resurrection (v35) and as they rehearse their story (v36- 'as they thus spake') the Lord Jesus appears in the middle of the room(v36). Despite His peace they think in their anxiety that they are seeing a spirit (v36-37) and to alleviate these concerns He invites them to touch Him to see that He is a real man (v38-40). The disciples were so amazed that they thought it was too good to be true ('believed not for joy' v41) and so He ate some fish and honey in front of them to prove that He was a real man and that He was alive (v41-43). The Lord then reminded them that He had previously told them He would rise from the dead. He had shown them from the Old Testament Scripture that the Messiah must rise again previously but He did it all over again starting at the beginning of the Bible showing the sufferings of Christ predicted for the Messiah and His glorious resurrection on the third day. (v44-46). He now proclaims that repentance and

he took bread, and blessed it, and brake, and gave
to them.
31 And their eyes were opened, and they knew him;
and he vanished out of their sight.
32 And they said one to another, Did not our heart
burn within us, while he talked with us by the way,
and while he opened to us the scriptures?
33 And they rose up the same hour, and returned to
Jerusalem, and found the eleven gathered together,
and them that were with them,
34 Saying, The Lord is risen indeed, and hath
appeared to Simon.
35 And they told what things were done in the way,
and how he was known of them in breaking of bread.

The Lord in the Midst of His Own

36 And as they thus spake, Jesus himself stood in
the midst of them, and saith unto them, Peace be
unto you.
37 But they were terrified and affrighted, and
supposed that they had seen a spirit.
38 And he said unto them, Why are ye troubled? and
why do thoughts arise in your hearts?
39 Behold my hands and my feet, that it is I myself:
handle me, and see; for a spirit hath not flesh and
bones, as ye see me have.
40 And when he had thus spoken, he shewed them
his hands and his feet.
41 And while they yet believed not for joy, and
wondered, he said unto them, Have ye here any
meat?
42 And they gave him a piece of a broiled fish, and
of an honeycomb.
43 And he took it, and did eat before them.
44 And he said unto them, These are the words
which I spake unto you, while I was yet with you,
that all things must be fulfilled, which were written
in the law of Moses, and in the prophets, and in the
psalms, concerning me.
45 Then opened he their understanding, that they
might understand the scriptures,

Ye are Witnesses

46 And said unto them, Thus it is written, and thus it

behoved Christ to suffer, and to rise from the dead
the third day:
47 And that repentance and remission of sins
should be preached in his name among all nations,
beginning at Jerusalem.
48 And ye are witnesses of these things.

The Ascension of the Lord Jesus

49 And, behold, I send the promise of my Father
upon you: but tarry ye in the city of Jerusalem, until
ye be endued with power from on high.
50 And he led them out as far as to Bethany, and he
lifted up his hands, and blessed them.
51 And it came to pass, while he blessed them, he
was parted from them, and carried up into heaven.
52 And they worshipped him, and returned to
Jerusalem with great joy:
53 And were continually in the temple, praising and
blessing God. Amen.

forgiveness of sins should be preached throughout the world and it starts with the disciples as witnesses (v47-48). They would be empowered shortly by the Holy Spirit (v49) at Pentecost (Acts 2).

24.50-53. He leads them out to the Mount of Olives as He ascends back to heaven with hands upraised as High Priest to bless them. He leaves the disciples worshipping in joy and waiting for the Holy Spirit to come to them. The gospel that starts with prayer and praise in the temple in chapters 1 and 2, ends with prayer and praise in the temple (v53).

Reflective Questions and Notes

A. What did the angels say to the women who came to the grave of Christ? (v5-6)

B. What convinced the women? (v6-8)

C. How did the disciples respond to the women's testimony? (v9-11)

D. What convinced the two on the road to Emmaus of His resurrection and the ten in the upper room? (v32, v44-48)

E. What do disciples have to do now? (v47-52)

____

____

____

____

____

Also available:

by C Munro:

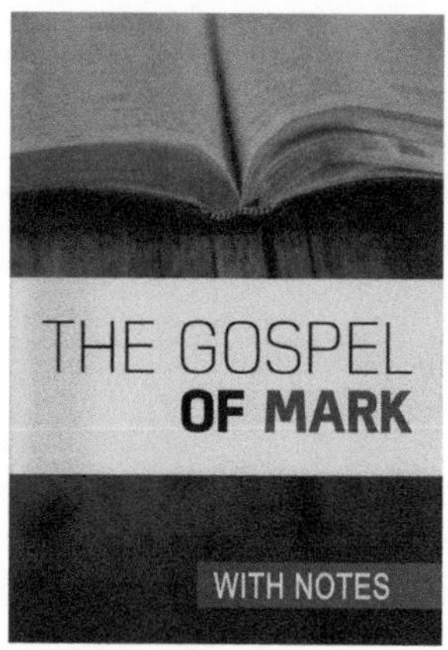

The Gospel of Mark

ISBN 9781910513590

Available from:

www.ritchiechristianmedia.co.uk

Also available:

by C Munro:

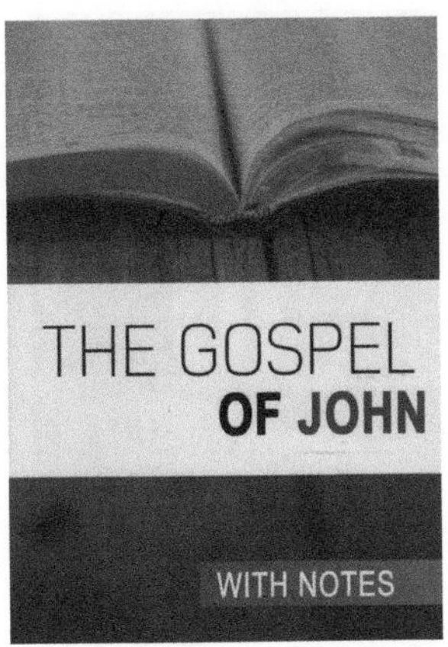

The Gospel of John

ISBN 9781910513729

Available from:

www.ritchiechristianmedia.co.uk

Also available:

by C Munro:

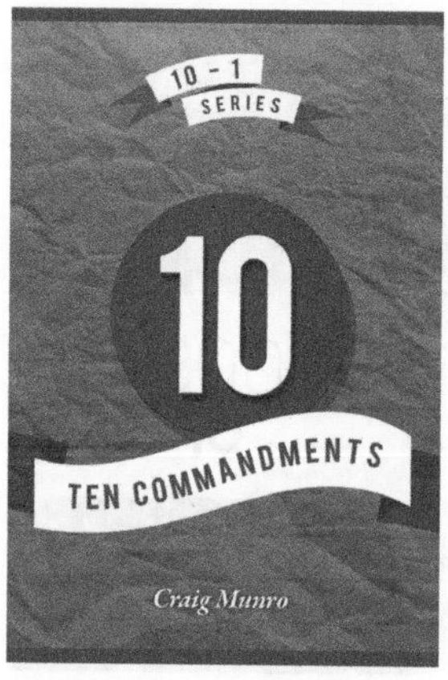

The Ten Commandments

ISBN 9781912522217

Available from:

www.ritchiechristianmedia.co.uk